KU-367-359

SHANTIES AND SAILORS' SONGS

STAN HUGILL

Shanties and
Sailors' Songs

with drawings by the author

HERBERT JENKINS
LONDON

© Stan Hugill 1969
All Rights Reserved

First published 1969 by
Herbert Jenkins Ltd
2 Clement's Inn, London WC2

SBN 257 65768 1

Printed in Great Britain by
Butler & Tanner Ltd
Frome and London

CONTENTS

ILLUSTRATIONS

PREFACE

This present volume has been compiled to give the serious student of folk-song of the sea, as well as the folk-club sea-song and shanty singer, a detailed coverage of the subject, both from the angle of literary research and from that of oral tradition.

My previous book, SHANTIES FROM THE SEVEN SEAS, covered the shanty field only. Within its pages, the origins, variants and foreign versions of hundreds of shanties will be found. This alone produced a formidable volume of 600 pages, in spite of much background material being jettisoned in favour of the texts.

When invited by Mr Leslie Shepard and the publishers to undertake the present work, I had some misgivings as to whether I could produce a book sufficiently different from my earlier one to justify its existence. However, as I researched, dipped into, collected and wrote, I found I was doing that which I thought at first impossible —the putting together, from an entirely new angle, of the songs and shanties of Sailor John. I accomplished this by producing a much wider and more detailed background to the sea-song and nautical ballad, by extending the choice of sea work-songs, by including material from coastwise ships, shipyards, sealers, and so forth, and enlarging the description of the cordage and ship furniture relevant to shantying. In the present work, I have included a few shanties not found in my previous work, but it is the inclusion of numerous examples of the non-working sea-song and, in particular, the naval sea-song, which makes this volume valuable and complementary to my SHANTIES FROM THE SEVEN SEAS.

My forefathers for several generations back, on both sides of the family, served in the two Services, Royal and Merchant Navy; one grandfather having been a warrant-officer in the old "Sailing Navy". My father was in the last of the naval sailing brigs and I myself managed to ship in the last of the British deep-water merchant sailing ships. I have mentioned these matters so that the reader will realise that I have been brought up in an atmosphere perfectly conducive to the imbibing and studying, consciously and unconsciously, of the songs of Jack Tar and Merchant John.

Many of the terms and phrases, mysterious to landsmen, found in the songs have here been translated and explained fully in simple language so that the folk-club singer and his audience will understand what the archaic sea-lingo and strangely "salt-waterfied" narratives of the songs are all about. I have endeavoured to correct many prevalent misconceptions and, by means of sketches and diagrams, I believe I have covered almost every query that may arise in the mind of the sea-song and shanty enthusiast.

I have included a chapter on twentieth-century sea-song and shanty collectors and editors, and also commented on some recent books and records available to the interested "folksonger". The bibliography, I hope, is sufficiently copious to satisfy the most avid enthusiast.

Within the last three years I have contacted many new pen-friends, people interested in the subject of sea-songs and shanties; and from these—from master mariner to landbound but sea-interested bank clerk—I have obtained much new material and have been given many new clues and pointers, the following up of which has brought fresh and often unique "fish" to my net. All these friends I must thank profusely. My thanks are also due to all the publishers, editors, collectors and seamen writers into whose books I have dipped so constantly. I must also thank the editors of the folk-song magazine SPIN for allowing me to use odds and ends first presented by me in my *Bosun's Locker* articles.

The music of most of the shanties was taken down from my singing by my brother Harold, now deceased, the tunes of those songs and shanties presented here for the first time were transcribed by Mr John Francis, B.A., of Aberdovey. Finally, I must thank Routledge and Kegan Paul Ltd for allowing me to use some of the shanties from my book SHANTIES FROM THE SEVEN SEAS in this present work.

And now, having prepared the ship for the voyage, let's cast off moorings and to sea. And to the reader and singer it's "Pleasant sailing!"

Stan Hugill

Aberdovey.

THE HISTORICAL BACKGROUND
OF THE SEA-SONG AND SHANTY

As I have declared many times in print, it is fairly certain that the seamen of the ancient world, those of the Middle Sea in particular, had chants of some kind which they would sing in order to keep in unison when rowing at the great sweeps of their biremes, triremes, pamphylians, penteconters and what not, but we have no printed record of them.

Fig. 1. Trireme

The drum was used of course, particularly in ships in which slaves and not freemen toiled at the oars, Songs of leisure, with a nautical flavour, must have circulated among these daring seamen, but here again, apart from one or two Greek manuscripts,[1] our knowledge of these is scanty.

From the days of the Vikings, through the Crusades of the twelfth

[1] OXYRHYNCHUS PAPYRI.

1

century, until the period of the Hanseatic "cogs" and Columbus's caravels and carracks of the fifteenth century, the tophamper in ships amounted to no more than the height of a single squaresail, with another squaresail fitted to the well-steeved bowsprit. Sometimes a triangular sail or lateen would be set on the poop. This type of rigging made work aloft almost negligible. Oars were not much used in merchant ships after Viking and Saxon times. However, war galleys continued to use them, particularly those of the Mediterranean countries, until the battle of Lepanto in 1571. This sea-fight, between the Moslem Turks and the combined fleets of Christian Spain and Italy, was the last great sea engagement under oars.

It was slowly becoming obvious that the sides of ships would be put to better use if pierced for guns instead of oars. In ships with oars, the main armament consisted of bow and stern chasers. By degrees, the canvas aloft was becoming more expansive. At the same time, the network of cordage for handling the ship grew more intricate. This obviously demanded a greater amount of "pulley-hauley". But did these old sea coneys sing a shanty on these new-fangled tackles? We cannot be sure with regard to earlier times, but we can guess that they did not haul the billowing, highly decorated topsails aloft mutely. We know for certain that they chanted some kind of running "sing-out" as they hand-over-hauled the working cordage. Wild, elemental yells they would be—the basis of all latter-day shantying.

The first mention in literature of the sing-out appears in a manuscript[2] of the time of Henry VI, in the year 1400 to be exact. The chronicler describes in detail the passage of a ship loaded with pilgrims making their way to the shrine of St James in Compostella, in Spain.

"Y-how! talia!" the remenaute cryen . . .

This refers to the sing-out. " 'Yo Ho! tail on the fall!' the rest sing out" could be its modern rendering. The manuscript from which these lines have been taken has been thought, by some authorities, to be the earliest sea-ballad to be found in print.

The next known evidence in literature relating to shantying, and

[2] THE EARLY NAVAL BALLADS OF ENGLAND, edited by J. O. Halliwell (the Percy Society, 1841).

Fig. 2. Hanseatic cog

in this case to the shantymen as well, is in the work of a Dominican friar, Felix Fabri,[3] who sailed aboard a Venetian galley on a passage to Palestine in the year 1493. Shantymen are described as "mariners who sing when work is going on . . . [There is] a concert between one who sings out orders and the labourers who sing in response..." The earliest work giving actual shanty verses is the COMPLAYNT OF SCOTLAND, of 1549. Two anchor songs are given, one bowline shanty, and three hauling songs for hoisting the lower yard. The form and language of these early shanties, apart from the fact that the English is Chaucerian, are very much like what our sailors of the sail sang three hundred years later.

For the seventeenth century, nothing as yet has turned up in "guid black prent" to prove whether or not shanties were sung in the ships of the Stuarts—ships which were, incidentally, a great improvement on their predecessors in both speed and sailing qualities.

Rowing songs, however, are often referred to in the literature of these times, many of these songs having the curious word "rumbelow" in their refrains. The sixteenth-century *Bowge at Court* has "Heve and how, rombelow, row the bote, Norman, rowe!" A book called THE YORKIST AGE, on life in the fifteenth century, describes the port of Bristol in these days and refers to "shanties echo-

[3] THE BOOK OF THE WANDERINGS OF THE BROTHER FELIX FABRI, translated by Aubrey Stewart (1893).

ing through the streets". A sailor song is given—I doubt if it is a
shanty—which follows:

> Hail and howe, rumbylowe!
> Steer well the ship and let the wind blow!
> Here cometh the Prior of Prikkingham and his convent,
> But ye keep the order well, ye shall be shent,
> With hail and howe . . .[4]

The word "rumbylowe" was known even in the early fourteenth
century. It occurs in the ballad-like verse on the Battle of Bannock-
burn (1314) which the chronicler Robert Fabyan quotes with the
comment "This songe was after many dayes sungyn, in daunces, in
carolis of the maydens and mynstrellys of Scotlande":

> Maydens of Englonde, sore maye ye morne,
> For your lemmans ye haue loste at Bannockisborne,
>   With heue a lowe.
> What wenyth the kynge of Englonde,
> So soone to haue wonne Scotlande
>   With rumbylowe.

William Dauney, in ANCIENT SCOTISH MELODIES (Edinburgh, 1838),
points out:

> 'Heve a lowe rumbelow' is said to be a sort of ancient chorus, but
> most commonly used by mariners. It is not unlike the modern
> 'yo-heave-o'. On this account, in the old song on Bannockburn,
> it is supposed to carry with it an allusion to King Edward's having
> escaped in a small skiff from Dunbar; or, as the loyal Caxton
> discreetly insinuates, 'forasmoche as he loved to gone by water'.

If the shanty field is sparse in evidence during the seventeenth
century, we have some pointers with regard to early sea-songs. The
famous old sea-ballad *The Lowlands Low* was popular at this time
and had, as the master of the ship concerned, Sir Walter Raleigh.
I doubt, however, if any of the present-day melodies of this song
would fit the original words. This ballad originated in the sixteenth
century, a period of discoveries and circumnavigators which one
would expect to be chock-a-block with nautical ballads. We know

[4] THE YORKIST AGE, by Paul Murray Kendall (George Allen and Unwin, 1962).

several did exist—sea-songs such as *Row Well, Ye Mariners*[5] and *The Sailor's Joy*—on account of their entries in the registers of the Stationers' Company (*c.* 1566), but they have failed to come down to us. *John Dory*, of the fifteenth century, and *Sir Andrew Barton*, a long-winded ballad of eighty-two verses, of the sixteenth century, we still have with us; the latter, under its more recent guise of *Henry Martin*, being popular in folk-song clubs even today.

It seems that men in the reign of Elizabeth I failed to sing of Drake and his contemporaries. Raleigh alone, of all the sea-dogs, made the grade—not as a seeker after Eldorado, but merely as a nasty ship's captain who refuses to allow a little cabin-boy to return to his ship after sinking the enemy. Some authorities suggest that it was a crafty printer, in the reign of Charles II, who planted Sir Walter's name into the already existing ballad of the *Lowlands Low*, and lowered his prestige somewhat.

By the seventeenth century the Spaniard, a traditional enemy of the Englishman who appeared in most sea-ballads, had been jettisoned in favour of the pirate; mainly the Barbary corsair or Sallee rover. From this period comes *High Barbary* or *Barbaree*, a song popular in any ship's fo'c'sle in the latter days of sail.

Its earliest form, called *The Saylor's Onely Delight*, ran:

> The *George Aloe* and the *Sweep-stake* too,
> *With hey, with hoe, for and a nony no!*
> Oh, they were merchant-men and bound for Safee.
> *And along the Coast of Barbary!*[6]

In this early version the French were the enemy—French pirates, that is—but in later versions a "salt-sea pirate" is the foe, and the ships become the *Prince of Luther* and *Prince of Wales*; such is the "folk process". It was often sung as a shanty in the nineteenth century. *The Bold Princess Royal*, a closely allied song, may also hark back to this period.

Probably the most famous of English naval ballads produced during these years (1630–55), however, is *Saylors For My Money*, by

[5] The tune of *Row Well, Ye Mariners* has survived, as it was used for a number of other ballads. It is printed in Thomas D'Urfey's WIT AND MIRTH; OR PILLS TO PURGE MELANCHOLY (1719–20), IV, p. 191) and used for the ballad *John and Joan*.

[6] ROXBURGHE BALLADS. A variant is to be found in Child's THE ENGLISH AND SCOTTISH POPULAR BALLADS (No. 285).

Martin Parker, to be found in the ROXBURGHE BALLADS. Its refrain runs: "How e're the wind doth blow." An adaptation of this ballad, *Neptune's Raging Fury*, was written about 1635. Whether this latter has any connection with the lost shanty bearing the same title and referred to by Dana in his TWO YEARS BEFORE THE MAST is rather doubtful:

> You gentlemen of England, that live at home at ease,
> Full little do you think upon the dangers of the seas;
> Give ear unto the mariners, and they will plainly show,
> The cares and fears *when the stormy winds do blow*[7]

This, in turn, was taken by Thomas Campbell (1800) and made into *Ye Mariners of England*, with another "windy" refrain:

> When the stormy winds do blow.[8]

Because of an embarrassment of abusive literature and ballads aimed at the Long Parliament, in the year 1649, Parliament passed an Act which banned all unlicensed books and pamphlets, while hawkers of ballads and ballad singers were ordered to be thrown into the House of Correction. This Act spelled death to the broadside ballad, and it was some years before the street ballad-makers got into their stride again.

At this point, it might be useful to say something about ballads.

Ballads, although not always historically true, colour and vivify the often only too dull contemporary records of history, enabling the historian to enrich his picture of the times with which he is dealing. In the sixteenth and seventeenth centuries, the ballad took the place of the modern newspaper, radio and television. Outstanding events of the day, the activities of royalty, wars, sports, suicides, murders and so on, were reported in song, and naturally, since we are an island race, verses on sea-fights, the ubiquitous press-gangs and Sailor John's roisterings were produced in abundance by the professional makers of broadsides. There is a technical difference, perhaps, between a ballad and a broadside. Leslie Shepard, in his book THE BROADSIDE BALLAD (H. Jenkins, 1962), points out that the

---

[7] ROXBURGHE BALLADS, Vol. VI.
[8] See Firth's NAVAL SONGS AND BALLADS (Navy Records Society, 1908).

traditional ballad stems from archetypal religious themes but the broadside ballad was mainly concerned with topical stories. There are black-letter and white-letter broadside ballads, printed on sheets of flimsy paper called broadsheets, and many of these are songs of ships and sailors. Some of the chapbooks of the eighteenth and nineteenth centuries too have songs of seafaring and seamen and the so-called slip-songs (narrow strip broadsheets) which followed them were very often sailor-songs.

Quite often, a broadside would be an adaptation of a prose pamphlet dealing with the same subject and, at times, the bookseller concerned would secure a copyright for a non-existing ballad version at the same time as he entered his prose pamphlet in the register of the Stationer's Company. In this way, he prevented rival publishers producing a ballad on the same incident, thus safeguarding the interest and sales of the original narrative.

A rough, not entirely reliable way of judging whether a sea-ballad is old (of the fifteenth, sixteenth or seventeenth century) or new (of the eighteenth or nineteenth century) is by the number of verses it contains. The older ones, generally speaking, have anything from fifteen to fifty verses; the newer ones from three to a dozen or so. The problem of discovering whether a sea-ballad is sailor-made or put together by a street ballad-maker is rather more difficult. I should say, however, that the majority of art-song writers and broadsheet authors were fond of including in their "sea" songs those references to classical mythology that seemed to fascinate the Englishman from the sixteenth century until Victorian times— Neptune, Triton, Remora, Venus, Cleophis, the Muses, the Atyx and so on. Such literary references, apart from Boreas (the North Wind), are very rarely, if ever, to be found in songs of shipboard manufacture.

By the second half of the seventeenth century, the "Butter-boxes" or "Hogan-Mogans", as the British Jack Tar derisively called the Holland Dutch, became the target of abuse in the ballad-makers' ditties. One of the best-known sea-ballads to have reached us from this era is the one which commences "To all you ladies now on land, we men at sea indite . . ." This was written, apparently, by the Earl of Dorset, although Samuel Pepys declares, rather ambiguously, that it was "made from the seamen at sea, to their ladies in town". The song, both the words and the music, is to be found in Chappell's

OLD ENGLISH POPULAR MUSIC, with another version in D'Urfey's PILLS TO PURGE MELANCHOLY.

Around the 1670s and 80s, Barbary pirate ballads once more became popular with Jack; such ballads as *The Algier Slave's Releasement*:

> Sometimes to the galleys I'm forced to go,
> Though amongst all my fellows like a slave I do row;
> And when I am spent with this labour and pain
> The thoughts of my love doth revive me again.[9]

From the late 1730s until 1815 and the defeat of Napoleon, England was at war with France and her allies, in addition to her struggle with her American colonists. It was an era when the ships and men of the Merchant Marine were overshadowed by those of the "King's Navee". The merchantmen of the time were, in the main, better armed and perhaps more disciplined than in earlier and later years. In fact, because of the stirring times, and the chance of being boarded or sunk by prowling privateers, pirates and continental *guerriers de course*, they emulated Big Brother in no small degree. To understand an eighteenth-century merchantman patterned faithfully on the Navy, we must have a "looksee" at an Honourable John East Indiaman.

Aboard these great, wall-sided, bluff-bowed plodders of the seas of Hindoostan, Cathay and Zipangu, naval traditions were carried out almost to a tee. Upper sails were furled at night and yards sent down on deck. Naval manœuvres, such as "reefing and going 'bout ship in one", were executed whenever possible. They had gunners, topmen, midshipmen, fifers, fiddlers, loblolly-boys, sweepers and other strange fish within their walls. The side was piped when the master came aboard, and all heaving and hauling was done to the sound of the fife, bosun's pipe and the calling of numbers, and gunnery practice was carried out daily. On a passage out to the Orient, if the East Indiaman cleared the Channel—the "Sea of Sick Heads and Sore Hearts"—without running foul of a "Johnny Crapoo" *coureur*, a Swedish privateer or, around the corner, one of the ships of Spain, she might not be so lucky with a sleek, oared and black-sailed galley of the Barbary corsairs, the Joassamee

---

[9] ROXBURGHE BALLADS, Vol. VII.

Fig. 3. Honourable John East Indiaman

pirates of the Indian coast, or the predatory junks of the Paracels and Bias Bay.

Of course, smaller and lesser-known types of merchantmen, although not such tempting prizes as Indiamen, also armed in case of attack. And even the smallest ship was over-manned compared to a sailing ship of a hundred years later. She had to be, so that in a chase canvas could be handled smartly and guns manned efficiently. So, with big crews and comparatively small ships, the need for work-songs would hardly arise. In the Navy it was usual—and still is for that matter—to "stamp away" with halyard falls. The men would grasp the rope and with their backs towards the job, so to speak, they would tramp up the deck, the men in front when they had "run their scope" dropping the no longer taut length of rope, and returning at a run to the tautened part near the lead-block. This process was repeated until the yard was mastheaded. At times, with big crews, two falls would be laid alongside each other and grasped—"marrying the falls", it was called—then twice as much weight could be lifted in one manœuvre. In the eighteenth century, this method of hauling was also met with ashore. Since it was also used by the members of various fire-fighting companies it was often referred to as a "fireman's walk".

Captain Whall,[10] and a few other authorities, seem to think that in revenue cutters and smaller fighting craft "stamp and go" songs

[10] SEA SONGS AND SHANTIES (Glasgow, 1910).

—the term used in merchantmen for this type of shanty—were permitted, although shantying was normally debarred in the Navy. *Drunken Sailor* and *Nancy Dawson* are given as the work-songs probably used, but there is no literary proof of this. *Nancy Dawson, Drops of Brandy* and *Off She Goes* were played by the fifers and fiddlers when heaving up the anchor aboard naval vessels, but there was no singing at this chore. In LANDSMAN HAY,[11] these tunes are mentioned as having been played at the capstan-head aboard H.M.S. *Culloden*. Here too, for the first time in print I should say, is to be found the expression "stamp and go", not in connection with halyards however, but in trundling round the capstan. As late as 1914, *Nancy Dawson* and *Drops of Brandy* were played by the ships' bands aboard naval ships during the daily issuing of rum. As well as these airs, many others were played aboard naval ships during the heaving of the anchor. I have found one instance of a shore-song being sung at the capstan. In the year 1665, the captain of the *Mary Galley* was accused of having purposely put his ship ashore on a rocky ledge outside Gloucester harbour in America. This trial was recorded in the MASSACHUSETTS ARCHIVE, and reference is made to the ship having been worked out of harbour on a Sunday morning. In order to encourage the men working at the windlass, they were told to sing while the drum kept the beat, and the song they sang was *The British Grenadiers*. In this case, however, I presume the ship would be a merchantman since the Thirteen Colonies had no naval ships until after 1776, when thirty merchantmen were converted into quasi-warships and called "naval". However, this incident does show how occasionally a song—not a shanty, be it noted—would be sung at work even aboard the iron-disciplined and navy-imitating merchantmen of those early days.

In fact, it can be assumed that aboard merchant ships of the late seventeenth and eighteenth centuries, shanties as we know them were markedly absent. There may have been cases where the discipline was lax and the occasional song allowed by the master—as in the case of the *Mary Galley*—but, if shantying was permitted, why is it absent from the printed page? Much time and energy have been spent by those interested in wading through the dusty literature of two hundred years ago vainly seeking early references

[11] MEMOIRS OF ROBERT HAY, 1789–1847, ed. by M. D. Hay (1953).

10

to shanty-singing. Some have thought that the song used in Shake-speare's *Tempest* may have been an early shanty:

> The Master, the Swabber, the Boatswain and I,
> The Gunner and his Mate,
> Lov'd Moll, Meg, and Marion and Margery,
> But none of us cared for Kate . . .

but there is no proof of this.

It is known that the great Elizabethan dramatist often purloined a folk-song to use in his works, and this song is also found in the NEW ACADEMY OF COMPLEMENTS (London, 1669), song no. 110. It has been suggested by C. H. Firth in NAVAL SONGS AND BALLADS[12] that a song called *The Benjamin's Lamentations* is from the reign of Charles II,

> Captain Chivers gone to sea,
> I boys, O, boys!

may have been an early shanty, but I doubt this. A sea-song having a "High boys, ho, boys!" or a "Yo, heave, ho!" refrain does not make it a shanty. The sea-songs of the period, those called by some writers art-songs as opposed to folk-songs, and many of the nautical ballads hawked around the streets by broadside sellers, were over-burdened with such refrains. In fact, as I have pointed out else-where, the famous "Yo, ho, ho!" with its piratical flavour was an almost unknown chorus in the shanty.

Recently, however, I came across one slender clue that may point to some form of shantying, or maybe to its forebear the sing-out, aboard a man-o'-war during the eighteenth century. This clue I have italicized in the following song, *The Jolly Sailor's True Description of a Man-of-War*. This broadside was printed and sold in Aldemary Churchyard, Bow Lane, London, and comes from DOUCE'S BALLADS, Vol. III. The first verses tell of the sailors and pressed men joining the ship, of the mustering and name-giving to the steward, followed by a description of work around the decks in preparation for sailing and the hoisting of yards ready for sea:

> Then up again upon the deck, so briskly, boys, we bundle;
> Since we have secur'd our pack, we have no cause to grumble.
> Then we clap on what we heave upon, some piping, *others*
> *singing*,
> There's hoist away, likewise belay, thus we make a beginning.

[12] Navy Records Society, 1908.

But on the other hand, this may be nothing more than the ballad-maker's choice of a rhyming word.

This period, however, even if it is devoid of any tangible evidence of shantying, saw the production and singing—in the theatre if nowhere else—of "artistic" sea-songs. They were the "pop" songs of those days of derring-do.

During the long years of the Napoleonic Wars, the naval Jack Tar was always in the public eye, and the theatre was one of the chief centres of his worship. In the main, however, the image offered to the public—that of a rubicund, fun-loving, saltwater-loving Jolly Jack Tar—was a false one.

Hearts of Oak apparently made its first appearance on the London stage in 1759, the melody by Dr Boyce and the words by the famous actor David Garrick. But the line "To honour we call you, not press you like slaves" was hardly appropriate at a time when press-ganging was the rule and not the exception. It was the only way in which seventy per cent of the King's Ships could be manned in times of war. The gangs, often referred to as the "Lobsters", scoured the whole countryside, inland towns and villages as well as seaports, lurking around crossroads, bridges and ferry-crossings. An old song, written during the American War of 1776, says that landsmen "for fear of the press won't lie in their beds".

Fear of impressment made able-bodied farmers send young boys and girls or old men to the markets instead of going themselves. In fact all landsmen between the ages of 15 and 55, in certain press-scoured districts, hid during the daylight hours so as to evade the gangs.

The "press" would invade the taverns, and even the churches, and there is a case in the ANNALS OF LIVERPOOL telling of how they entered the Customs House of this port after their victim. In 1710, East India House in Leadenhall Street, London, was also invaded by the "Lobsters". When men were short, even cripples would be pressed into service. The lieutenants in charge of the gangs, usually referred to as "Yellow Admirals", were in the main a crafty and villainous lot. They would accept bribes from well-to-do pressed men, and many grew rich on "cooking the footage" (making out that they had travelled twice as far as they really had on their predatory excursions). They would also invent lists of non-existent pressed men in order to claim their victualling allowances. This latter trick was also common among naval pursers in those days, so much so that they had to lodge a sum of money with the Admiralty as a guarantee against appropriating goods entrusted to their care.

Few art-songs of the period sing of the predatory press-gangs. Some folk-songs, however, telling of such acts as the pressing of a poor sailor about to be married, with the hapless bride-to-be left crying on the steps of the church, or of the rousing of the poor victim from his marriage bed, have come down to us, mainly from the north-east coast area.

> The very first day I got married,
> That night as I lay on my bed,
> A press-gang broke into my bedroom,
> And these words to me they was said.
>
> Arise from your bed my young rooster,
> And then come along quick with me,
> To the far Lowlands of Holland,
> To face the enemy.

William Taylor is one of these songs that has stood the test of time and is still sung around the folk-song clubs:

> William Taylor was a brisk young sailor,
> He who courted a lady fair,
> Bells were ringin', sailors singin'
> As to church they did repair.
>
> Thirty couples at the wedding,
> All were dressed in rich array;
> Instead of William being married,
> He was pressed and sent away.

Captain Bover appears to have been one of the most hated press-gang masters on the north-east coast. Laura Smith, in her book THE MUSIC OF THE WATERS, quotes:

> Where hes ti' been, maw canny hinny,
> Where has ti' been, maw winsome man?
> Aw've been ti' the norrard, cruisin' back an' forrard,
> Aw've been ti' the norrard, cruisin' sair and lang,
> Aw've been ti' the norrard, cruisin' back and forrard,
> But daurna come ashore for Bover and his gang.

A sailor-composed ditty called *The Greenland Men*, said to have been put together by eighteen Greenlanders down in the hold of the *Swan* tender in Leith Roads in 1778, has the following stanza:

We're now on board the *Jenny*, to Glasgow she is bound,
And to secure us from the press we landed in a Highland sound.

(From PORTSMOUTH JACK'S GARLAND)

The press-gang tender, it would appear, was often cruising around other places as well as "of the Bar o' Shields". In fact these tenders or press-smacks would meet homeward-bound merchant ships off the Nore, in the Downs, or off Spithead, board them and press into service the most able-bodied seamen, leaving the ships so short of hands that they were virtually "all adrift". East Indiamen were issued with 'protections' by the Admiralty, but even these failed to save them from being boarded. There is one recorded instance of a well-armed East Indiaman fighting and beating a man-o'-war which was out to impress the merchantman's crew. It was this pressing of the homeward-bound merchant seamen—men who had been away for months, if not years, living on salt junk only, without a speck of chlorophyll in sight—that caused the disastrous spread of scurvy among the crews of the old first-raters and lesser fry. It was, perhaps, this impressment of merchant seamen that was one of the contributory causes of the lack of shantying aboard merchant ships at this time. Naturally, the best seamen were chosen by the press-gangs and these would include the shanty-men. They would be away for years in a service in which shantying was taboo. The vacant places aboard the merchant ships would be filled by the poorest specimens of landsmen and foreigners the crimps of the period could find, men who knew nothing of shanties or shantying.

The street broadside vendors churned out many press-gang ballads, of which the following are good examples:

But when they were going in at the church door,
A press-gang did meet them, 'twas near to a score;
Instead of being married, he was pressed away,
So nothing was there but a sorrowful day.

(*The Sailor's Misfortune*—Ashton, REAL SAILOR SONGS)

Cruel was the press-gang as tore my love from me,
And cruel was the wind as it bore him off to sea,
And cruel was the captain and the bosun and the men,
And cruel was our parting if we never meet again.

(The Press-gang)

Now when her father came to know,
His daughter lov'd this young man so,
He caus'd him to be prest to sea,
To keep her from his company.

(The Ship Carpenter's Love to the Merchant's Daughter—Ashton)

Farewell our wives and dearest children,
Our friends and relations we must bid adieu,
For the press-gang they have press'd us,
For to fight our daring foe.

(Press'd Man's Lamentations—Ashton)

During the reign of William III, impressment was looked upon, by everyone but the poor devils pressed, as a rather patriotic affair. One ballad from this period tells how an array of six lusty maids form their own press-gang, and go about the streets of London impressing tailors. Tailors, for some unknown reason, in all forms of folk-song, are treated as less than men and were always supposed to have lecherous natures. In this ballad, the maids impress fourteen of them.

With all might and main down to Dutchy Lane,
These petticoat press-masters hurried again.
To press some they knew; 'twas Morgan and Hugh,
A couple belong'd to the cross-legged crew,
And Welsh tailors.

(The Maiden's Frolic—ROXBURGHE BALLADS, Vol. III)

From the sailor's point of view (or perhaps it was that of the street ballad-maker), William IV was looked upon as the chap responsible for the easing of impressment and flogging. According to the following song, when he was a duke he got himself pressed in order to find out all about the system. We know he did sympathise with the hardships of a sailor's life, but whether he went to this extreme is highly debatable.

15

Then upstairs they did go, and in a room did enter,
The Duke did say, Landlady, please bring wine both white and
                                                              red:
Before the wine was drunk out, a press-gang bold and stout
In the lower rooms for sailors bold did look and search about.

Aboard ship after having been pressed, Duke William had to strip, ready for the bosun's mate to flog him. William says:

No wonder my royal father cannot man his shipping,
'Tis by using them so barbarously, and always them a-whipping,
But, for the future, sailors all, shall have good usage,
To hear the news, together all cried, May God bless Duke
                                                              William!

(*Duke William's Frolic*—John Ashton, MODERN STREET BALLADS)

After 1815, impressment ceased, petered out slowly and, by 1835, although not formally abolished was finished for ever.

Returning to the art-songs of those days, we find that shore-composed sea-songs and ballads, based on the supposed rollicking life and loves of robust Jack Tar, inundated the contemporary scene. In the main, such songs sang of his sweethearts, his sea-fights, his customs (naval), his seamanship and the gales he encountered, in that order. During the seventeenth and eighteenth centuries, there were numerous narrative ballads based on some female, real or imaginary, who follows her sailor lover to sea in the guise of a sea-man. *Susan's Adventures in a Man-of-War* is one good example, as is *The Female Cabin Boy*:

'Tis of a handsome female, as you may understand,
She had a mind for rovin', unto a foreign land;
Attired in sailor clothing she boldly did appear,
And engaged with a captain for to serve him for a year.

Hannah Snell, who in 1750 signed as a soldier and eventually went to sea aboard a man-o'-war, has several ballads woven around her adventurous career. It is not generally realised, however, that women were often found in the crew of a naval vessel. They were mainly engaged in the cockpit or powder magazines handling the ammunition. Queen Victoria appears to have put a stop to women going to sea, "powder-monkeys" (small boys) being employed instead.

Songs telling of "tokens", whole rings and half rings, binding lovers separated by the "wild waves" were also much to the fore in those days. Some became popular with the lower-deck—*Fair Phoebe* and *The Dark-eyed Sailor* are two—and were sung on Saturday night: the one night a week in the old "Sailing Navy" (and in the more modern Navy, too) when merry songs and toasts lifted the beams of the deckhead.

Songs of Lovely Nancy, Pretty Polly and Blackeyed Susan were great favourites—"Nancy" ballads probably outnumbering the others.

> Farewell, my lovely Nancy, since I must now leave you,
> Unto the salt seas I am bound for to go . . .

> Farewell, my lovely Nancy, no longer can I stay,
> Our tops'ls are hoisted, and the anchor's aweigh,
> And our ship lies waiting in a fast and flowing tide,
> And if I ever return again I will make you my bride.

Other songs woven around a Nancy are *The Bristol Wedding*, *The Sailor Bold* and *The Tarry Sailor*.

Charles Dibdin (1745–1814), the great naval balladeer of the eighteenth century, wrote:

> Your Polly has never been false she declares,
> Since the last time we parted at Wapping Old Stairs . . .

which, besides singing of the sailor's girl, gives us a glimpse of the happy custom of the time of permitting women, mainly loose women, to board ships down at Gravesend, the Nore and the Downs. Pressed men, being unable to go ashore in case they absconded, were allowed bumboats alongside with the Jewish slop-dealers bringing them tobacco, clothing and booze, not to mention harlots from the Ratcliffe Highway.

> When I passed a whole fortnight atween decks with you,
> Did I ere give a kiss, lad, to one of your crew?

John Gay's (1685–1732)

> All in the Downs the Fleet lay moored,
> When Blackeyed Susan came aboard[13]

[13] This ballad and *Admiral Benbow* were both delivered by well-known singers from the rotundas of the eighteenth-century London pleasure gardens of Ranelagh and Vauxhall.

is another song which, in an innocuous way, touches on this old-time custom of women being allowed in the 'tween-decks of men-o'-war.

A rather more factual song is the following, which tells of the old naval custom of signifying that the ship was open to port wenches by draping the tumble-home sides of a man-o'-war with red-dyed cordage, and hanging from the gun-ports red petticoats swiped from previous ship-visiting harlots.

> No more the waves and winds will sport,
> Our vessel is arrived in port;
> At anchor see she safely rides,
> And gay red ropes adorn her sides.
> Her sails are furled, her sheets belayed,
> The crimson petticoats displayed.
> Deserted are our useless shrouds,
> And the wenches come aboard in crowds.
>
> Then come, me lads, a quick foot round,
> While safely moored on English ground.

It was this custom of allowing the port wenches aboard that started the well-known turning-out cry of "Show a leg!" The seamen of those days went bare-footed, whereas the women who came aboard sported white cotton stockings. Hence, when the bosun's mate made his rounds in the morning to turn the hands to, his cry of "Show a leg!" would produce either a bare calf or a white-stockinged leg—the former having to jump out of their hammocks smartly, the ladies being allowed to lie in.

While on this subject, I would like to point out something about which I, along with many of the best folk authorities, have been in ignorance. It has always seemed to any student of eighteenth-century pseudo-naval songs that the constantly recurring sailor names, such as Ben Backstay, Tom Bowling, Jack Mainyard, Sam Spritsail, Ned Junk, Jack Block and so on, were purely figments of the imagination of patriotic dramatists and song-writers of the day. However, in recent times, I have come across proof that this was not so.

This permitting of women aboard naval ships naturally led, in many cases, to babies being conceived "on the breech of a gun". To explain this, the reader must bear in mind that when these eighteenth-century ships were built, no allowance would be made for living quarters for the men before the mast. They hung their hammocks above the guns and the area between the guns was the only place allotted to Jolly Jack in which to keep his belongings. So when these women came on board they had to keep to the areas between the guns. Scenes of wild abandonment and drunken orgies were a feature of those times and, usually, the sex act was performed on the gun or alongside it. Hence, a sailor "born to the sea" was defined in the old sea-lingo as "Begotten in the galley and born under a gun. Every hair of his chest a ropeyarn, every finger a fish-hook, and every drop of his blood Stockholm tar". The expression "son of a gun" used to this day with a slightly different meaning, meant a man conceived in this fashion—a bastard, in other words. The names these "sons of guns" took were actually parts of the rigging of the ship. Hence Ben Backstay, Tom Bowling, and so on, were actual people. Tom Bowling, for example, we know to have been a true "son of a gun". He went ashore once from a ship in which he served seventeen years. He died of gun wounds in 1790 and was buried at Haslar, near Portsmouth.

Although it was a period of the lash, of press-gangs, of poor diet and iron discipline while at sea, hardship or cruelty is rarely found in the art-songs of the period. Seldom does one come across a street ballad telling of the viciousness of sea punishments,[14] and even the true sailor songs—naval as opposed to those of the merchant seaman—that speak of such are but a handful in number. One, obviously sailor-composed, harking back to the early 1800s and still extant, which depicts truthfully the hazing common in the Royal Navy, is that called *The Flash Frigate* or *La Pique*:

'Tis of a flash frigate, *La Pique* was her name,
All in the West Indies she bore a great name;
For cruel bad usage of every degree,
Like slaves in the galley we ploughed the salt seas.

So now, brother shipmates, where'er ye may be,
From all fancy frigates I'd have ye steer free;
For they haze ye, and flog ye till ye ain't worth a damn,
Then ship ye half-dead to yer own native land.

[14] Leslie Shepard has an unusually outspoken broadside against flogging, with the title *Lay of the Lash* (mentioned in the magazine SING, Vol. 2, No. 3, Aug.–Sept. 1955, p. 48).

I learned this from a ditty-box songbook handed down from my grandfather, the yellow pages of which contain many salty old ballads carefully entered in his beautiful copperplate handwriting. Another naval song in similar vein, sung to the tune of a once-popular capstan shanty, *Jamboree*, is *Aboard of the Man-o'-war*:

> They hung me up by my two thumbs,
> And they slashed me till the blood did run;
> They cut a net crosst me back an' bum,
> O! aboard of the man-o'-war!

Such songs, however, date from the period following the Peace of 1815, when a new form of discipline, that of "spit and polish", grew apace, and the martinet came into his own. Singing of these martinets—the name, by the way, comes from an old term for the cat-o'-nine-tails—a sailor-composed ballad suggests that the ladies o' town should give him a "going-over".

> But when on shore the bully comes, if with him you should
>   fall in,
> The whore that gives him a drubbing shall have a gown and a
>   gallon of gin.

(*The Vanguard*, from C. H. Firth's NAVAL SONGS AND BALLADS)

These three truthful ballads stand out like sore thumbs among the spate of hundreds of untruthful ones which glorify the naval sailor and give a false impression of life afloat in the "King's Navee". Songs of the true-blue type of sailor were plentiful:

> 'Tisn't the jacket an' trousers blue, nor the song and the grog
>   so cheerily,
> That shows the heart of a seaman true, or tells of his manners
>   sincerely;
> But 'tis the hour of strife, when venturing his life,
> When misfortune an' trouble assail her,
> In battle he'll sing for Britannia and King,
> That shows us the heart of a sailor.

and how about

> In storms when clouds obscure the sky,
> And thunders roll and light'nings fly,
> In midst of all these dire alarms,
> I think my Sally on thy charms,

The troubled main, the wind and rain,
My ardent passion prove,
Lashed to the helm, should seas o'erwhelm,
I think on thee my love.

A rather fanciful picture of Jack tied to the wheel, dreaming of his girl friend instead of concentrating on the caution: "Meet her bully, when she rolls!" Thanks to Sally, both the helmsman and the ship would soon find themselves in one hell of a mess.

Although nautical ballads had always been intended to bring to the landlubber the ways of the seaman, it wasn't until the beginning of the eighteenth century that men of letters began to write them and offer them a higher class of listener. Such popular nautical ballads as Shields' (1670–1738) *The Heaving of the Lead*, first sung in the operatic farce HERTFORD BRIDGE, and the *Saucy Arethusa*, an ancient melody, probably from O'Carolan (1670–1738), adapted by Shields with words by Prince Hoare and first sung in a comedy called LOCK AND KEY on a London stage; Alan Cunningham's (1784–1842) *Wet Sheet and a Flowing Sea*; Richard Brinsley Sheridan's (1751–1816) *Come Sling the Flowing Bowl*, and Dibdin's *Tom Bowling* and *Anchor's Weighed*, cannot compare with the tough and often coarse forebitters of the late eighteenth and nineteenth centuries; true sea-songs from unknown sailor authors. In fact, the so-called "come-all-ye's" of the sixteenth, seventeenth and eighteenth centuries seem to be nearer to these latter than do the art-songs, many of which are full of wrongly used nautical terms and of landsmen's ideas of sea-talk, since they were "composed" by the ballad-makers and sold as broadsides in the streets of London. As for their tunes, these were usually "pinched" from older songs, the name of the air being printed at the head of the broadsheet.

A song my grandfather and father both used to sing is a "come-all-ye" of early date which has alternate stanzas of irreproachable seamanship, appearing to have been written by a seaman, but with the remaining verses, seemingly, of "art" origin. This curious song, sometimes called *The Tempest, Rude Boreas* or *The Storm*, is said to have been popularised by G. A. Stevens in 1754. I have always believed, wrongly perhaps, that this song, viewed from its seamanship, was of a very early date, but its inclusion of staysails has caused me to date it no earlier than the 1730s. Fore-and-aft sails, in the shape of lateens, were favoured by the Arabs, Phoenicians, Byzantines and even the Portuguese of the sixteenth century, but from then onwards the rig died out in favour of the better-cut square-sails, and did not appear again in big ships until the introduction of jibs, staysails and gaff-sails roughly around the beginning of the eighteenth century. Bomb ketches and smaller craft, however, began to use triangular sails in preference to the spritsail on their bow-sprits in the late seventeenth century. Even then, they did not come into general use, for instance in the East Indiamen, until the mid or later eighteenth century. Since this song could be considered a "missing link" between art-songs, phoney "come-all-ye's" and sailor-composed songs, I have decided to give it in full on page 220.

One has only to wade through any collection of nautical ballads of this period to learn that songs of gales and wrecks are plentiful, and of sea-fights even more so. Generally speaking, however, these are not the voice of the sailor. From the time of the Armada onwards, nautical ballad-makers did a thriving trade. Whether sailors actually sang these shore-composed ballads it is impossible to say; somehow or other, I have my doubts. Some of the better ones, such as *Admiral Benbow*—the one with the *Captain Kidd* tune—may have been fairly well aired, although I'm inclined to agree with Captain Whall that it was in the ward-room, rather than among the men, that such ditties would be sung. The man-before-the-mast or the "lower-decks" probably preferring to sing "pop" shore songs, that is those having nothing to do with the sea. Touching on Captain Kidd brings us to those long, rambling ballads of pirates and buccaneers. But here again, their words savour of shore-manufacture rather than of sea-grown songs.

Around the beginning of the eighteenth century, new-style pirate songs took the place of the earlier ones referring to the Sallee rovers. The pirates found in these songs were those of the eastern seas rather than those of the Spanish Main and Barbary Coast; villains who had their headquarters in Madagascar. Kidd, who was hanged at Execution Dock in 1701, was one of these, and his rather lugubrious and long-winded ballad, *Captain Kid's Farewel to the Seas* (*sic*), was whittled down by later seamen and is still very popular with folk-singers of today. The original ran:

My name is Captain Kid, who has sail'd, who has sail'd,
My name is Captain Kid, who has sail'd.

My name is Captain Kid, what laws I still forbid,
Unluckily I did, while I sail'd, while I sail'd.

This unique example of the song is reprinted from Firth's NAVAL
SONGS AND BALLADS, who in turn had it from the collection of Lord
Crawford. The more modern version, of course, has "as I sailed, as
I sailed" for the repeated refrain. The *Death of Admiral Benbow* was
later cast in the same metre and sung to a similar tune.

Come all ye seamen bold, lend an ear, lend an ear,
Come all ye seamen bold, lend an ear,
'Tis of our Admiral's fame,
Brave Benbow was his name,
How he fought all on the main, you shall hear, you shall hear,
How he fought all on the main, you shall hear.

Another Benbow ballad, rather a favourite with seamen even
until the late 1800s, starts "We sailed from Virginia and thence to
Fayal . . ." It is given with its tune in Whall's SEA SONGS AND SHANTIES.

Captain Avery, another notorious Madagascar pirate, is said to
have composed the following ballad about himself. In it he calls
himself "Every". The full ballad is to be found in THE PEPYS
COLLECTION.

Come all you brave boys, whose courage is bold,
Will you venture with me ? I'll glut you with gold,
Make haste unto Corona, a ship you will find,
That's called the *Fancy*, will pleasure your mind.

The tune to which the ballad was sung is *The Two English Travellers*.

The villain Teach, or Blackbeard, apparently had no ballads
about his misdeeds,[15] but one does exist about Lieutenant Maynard
who killed the pirate in an action in James River, Virginia, 1718.

The so-called common seaman of those days was rather low in
mental capacity, often brutalised, usually half-starved, exhibiting
mainly animal instincts and frequently illiterate. Even in the second
half of the nineteenth century and later, many seamen signed on a
ship by "making their mark", being unable to read or write. This
lack of learning, however, did not prevent shore rustics from turning out folk-songs, and neither would it have prevented seamen, in

[15] Except for the precocious broadside piece by Benjamin Franklin, written when
only a boy.

a similar case, from producing songs about their sort of life. Nevertheless, a spate of good songs could hardly have been expected to issue from the majority of these fo'c'sle hands. Among the pressed men, however, there would be some who were better educated. These men, although at first ignorant of the ways of ships and the sea, would, after five years or more in one of His Majesty's frigates, be well capable of producing sailor songs, good in both composition and sailor-like qualities. The few sea-songs, containing irreproachable nautical terms and phrases, that have come down to us are, undoubtedly, the work of such seamen. These sailor-made ballads often contain in the last stanza a statement such as:

> I am a saucy foremast Jack,
> To the *Arrow* I belong.

or

> So now to conclude and finish my song,
> I am a saucy mizen-top man, to the *Vanguard* I belong.

Some of the sailor-composed songs, dating from the Napoleonic Wars, were made by war-crippled and blinded seamen who sang them to obtain charity from passers-by in the streets of Wapping, in London. Their final verses are usually of the following kind:

> I'm blind and I'm a cripple, yet cheerful would I sing,
> Were my disasters triple, 'cause why? 'twas for my king.

> . . . by hard fortune you plainly see,
> We lost our limbs on the raging sea,
> All you who extend your charity,
> The Lord preserve your family.

(From the *Seaflower*)

Ill-fed and underpaid, iron-disciplined and severed from the gaieties of shore life, a song was one of the very few comforts a naval seaman was permitted. But here again, when at sea, most singing had to be executed *sotto voce*. It is interesting to point out here that two hundred years later aboard the Finnish grain ships trading to Australia, singing around the decks was considered by their officers a mark of poor discipline, and was, in most Finnish ships, forbidden.

We have already noted how the hammock and the gun beneath it was the naval seaman's only "home". In battle, the hammock part of his "home" was triced up in the shrouds or in the hammock-nettings to act as sandbags did in the trenches of World War I. At sea, obviously, discipline saw to it that quiet at all costs was the order in the 'tween decks. Nevertheless, contemporary writers describe how, in harbour when the port women were aboard, discipline was relaxed and the noise of the sex-starved sailors and their strident-voiced harlots, along with the raucous singing by both of obscene songs, was something repellent to any sensitive-eared land-lubber.

Sea-punishments in these times were really vicious. Flogging, at the gangway, or grating, or in the rigging, was common in the Navy. Flogging around the fleet was rarer but still far too common. The man under punishment was lashed to handspikes athwart the gunnels of the ship's longboat, and then rowed from ship to ship of the Grand Fleet, the victim being flogged at each ship's gangway by the bosun or his mate. Before the whole gauntlet was run, the man usually died, but to conform to the regulations, the remaining strokes had to be carried out on the corpse. In 1879, the number of lashes, hitherto unlimited, was ordered to be twenty-five. Naval punishments were based on the ancient Laws of Oleron, which were instituted by the King of Castille, Alphonso X, in the thirteenth century. These were copied from the Marine Code of the Romans, which in turn had come from the sea-laws of the Island of Rhodes and from the Codes of the maritime cities of the Mediterranean. The Laws of Oleron ordered a shipboard murderer to be bound to his victim's corpse and dumped overboard. Boiling pitch was poured over the head of shipboard thieves. In the reign of Henry VIII and later, a seaman found asleep on watch was mastheaded and water poured down his sleeves. This was done in Nelson's day and known as "grampussing". For the fourth such offence, the culprit was hung in a cage from the bowsprit with a knife, a loaf of bread and a can of beer. Then he would have to choose one of two deaths, either slow starvation or cutting the rope by which he was hung to the bowsprit and thereby drowning himself. Keelhauling, although occasionally resorted to in the British Navy, was really a Dutch punishment. It died out in British ships somewhere around 1740. Yardarm hanging of course was the usual finish to a mutineer.

The last one in the British Fleet took place in Talienwan ("Tally-and-One" Sailor John called it) Bay in the Second Chinese War, of 1860.

Some say that there must have been a happier side to a naval seaman's life. What about the "Dance and Skylark" or "Song and Skylark" interlude in the dog-watch?

This period of entertainment for the men was that of the second dog-watch; from 6 to 8 p.m. It was a naval custom matched in the Merchant Service by the unorganised "playtime" of the fo'c'sle-hands when they would have some merriment, playing instruments in their homemade "fufu" band, or singing the so-called forebitters or songs of leisure.

In the Navy however, this period was an organised one, being originally instituted as a means to prevent that cursed sickness of the sailing ship, scurvy. The false belief was that the more a man moved his body the less likely he was to contract such illness, movement causing the red corpuscles to chase the white ones out of the system. This of course, was before the introduction of limejuice. Far from being a free period of rest and play, it was an order from my Lords of the Admiralty, and the men had to dance the hornpipe

Fig. 4. The Hornpipe

and, I believe in the earlier ships, the saraband, whether they liked it or not. The ship's fiddler would accompany the dancing of the men, and he, incidentally, in those days, was signed on the ship's book not as a musician but as a member of the sick bay. In fact he and the hornpipe could be called anti-scorbutics ! There were, however, some similarities to the merchant seaman's dog-watch leisure. Pipes and "chawing tobaccy" would be allowed the men, and singing, too, was a feature of the Navy "Dance and Skylark". The "skylarking" would be rough, and the pigtailed matlows would often indulge in vicious physical "games". But these, too, were played under the eye of the officers. It was hardly a period of relaxation as it was in the Merchant Service.

In the seventeenth and eighteenth centuries, so far as I'm aware, censorship of street ballads was non-existent. And since unwholesome murders, assaults, suicides, fires, riotings and such like were the stuff of which the broadsides were made, one would naturally expect broadsides in a nautical vein and sea-songs of the period to include at least some of the harrowing experiences and vicissitudes the men of the old wooden walls had to endure; but no ! There seems to have been, in the main, a curtain of silence drawn over such matters. Perhaps the reason for this was that owing to England being in a constant state of war, the street singers felt that they had to glorify the Navy rather than tell the truth, and patriotically sing of its good side rather than about flogging and keelhauling. Even the famous Mutiny of the Nore (1797) has little in song, and certainly truth is absent from the one mutiny ballad I have seen. This mutiny, led by a seaman called Parker, who was subsequently hanged from the yardarm, was the outcome of poor (often nonexistent) pay, the fiddling of the victuals by the scurvy type of purser already mentioned, the surfeit of flogging for the mildest sins, as well as many other raw deals the sailor had heaped on his back in those days. Yet, little of this is brought forth in song.

In Masefield's A SAILOR'S GARLAND is to be found one of the few Mutiny songs. It is sung to the tune of *The Vicar of Bray*, and is called *A New Song on Parker the Delegate*. From its content, it is fairly obviously a shore ballad-maker's effort to appease the powers and not the sailors. Strangely enough, the sentiments it contains are somewhat comparable to those of a larger part of the powers and public with regard to the seamen's strike in 1966. Apropos strikes, it is thought that the "striking" of the yards (the lowering of the yards to the gunnels) so as to prevent the fleet sailing in the Nore Mutiny gave rise to the use of the word in its present-day meaning of a stoppage of work. Here is the opening stanza of the song:

I will not sing in Parker's praise, disgraceful is the story,
Nor yet to seamen tune my lays, eclipsed is now their glory.
Fell Faction's head they proudly rear 'gainst their country and
'gainst king, sir,
And on this land they now do try destruction for to bring, sir.
Then Britons all, with one accord, fight for your Constitution,
And let surrounding foes behold we want no revolution.

Another ballad, more popular with the seamen no doubt, is *The
Death of Parker*. This tells in a fairly factual way how, after the hanging of Parker from the yardarm and his disgracefully speedy inter-
ment, his widow and two female friends in the dead of night went to
the burying-ground. Here, they dug up the corpse with their bare
hands, then took the body to London where they gave it a more
decent burial.

Although the ballads of the period appear to be, in the main,
against Parker and the seamen, a nineteenth-century chapbook does
contain a rather more truthful narrative of the trial of "Richard
Parker, President of the Delegates for Mutiny".

During the long wars with the French, the naval sailor grumbled,
rightly so, over impressment, long cruises and stoppage of shore
liberty, over unscrupulous pursers, lack of pay, transferment from
one ship to another without wages so that seamen had to sell their
pay-tickets to slimy ticket-buyers for half-price, bad grub and vile
punishments.

The Sea Martyrs, a ballad preserved by Pepys, tells us something of
the story—of lack of pay and so on—but not in as forceful language
as was later used by the merchant packet seamen when singing of
their hardships.

Their starving families at home
Expected their slow pay would come . . .

Their poor wives with care languished,
Their children cried for want of bread,
Their debts increase. . . .

When these naval seamen sent a deputation to Whitehall to ask for
their long overdue pay they were made to suffer the death penalty
as mutineers :

What times are these ! Was't ever known,
'Twas death for men to ask their own.

28

and   To robbers, thieves and felons they
Freely grant pardon every day;
Only poor seamen, who alone
Do keep them on their father's throne
Must have at all no mercy shown;
Nay, tho' there wants fault, they'll find one.

Another seventeenth-century ballad about the awful food served out by the unscrupulous and thieving pursers still exists. This is in rather more forceful language than usual for the times. It is called *The True Character of the Purser of a Ship*, and some of the more potent lines run:

Of all the curst plagues that e'er Fate did decree,
To vex, plague and punish her sailors at sea,
There's none to compare with the purser, that evil
Who's worse than a jailor, a bum, or a devil,
Sure when he was framed Dame Nature lay dying,
Hell then took a purge, Hell then took a purge
And Pluto shit him flying.

As his name foully stinks, so his butter rank doth smell . . .

Then our urine to purge, that the men may piss clear,
Instead of what's better, his petty-warrant beer
Is by him allowed . . .

His oatmeal, or grout, known by the name burgooe,
Is fitting for nothing but make a sailor spew . . .

As for oatmeal and peas we never got any of that,
Our purser—puts 'em in his pocket to make his guts fat.

                        (C. H. Firth's NAVAL SONGS AND BALLADS)

According to the *Ticket Buyer's Lamentations*, from a broadside in the possession of C. H. Firth, the practice of naval seamen selling their pay-tickets for half-price to the usurers (in the manner of merchant seamen in later days when wishing to cash their "advance notes") began to be checked. This occurred around the middle of the eighteenth century when the Admiralty, at long last, decided to begin paying the seamen regularly each month.

An usurer in Lothbury, a Jew of high renown,
Hearing the sailors would be paid strait hasted up to town.
What! pay the Navy all, d'you say, sure that can never be!
For then much greater men must lose their trades as well as
                                   we . . .

Samuel Pepys died in 1703. He was responsible for much of what we know about the naval matters and sea-ballads of those days. Unfortunately, no one took his place as a collector of such things, so that during the reign of Queen Anne, many nautical ballads were allowed to perish through the lack of interest shown in sea matters.

In naval ships engaged in exploration and circumnavigation during the eighteenth century, discipline was supposedly relaxed a little. Often the ships themselves were merchantmen, requisitioned by the Navy. This was true in the case of Captain Cook's ship, and also in that of Bligh's *Bounty*. Cook's *Endeavour* was a fairly happy ship, but as everyone knows, this was not so in the case of the *Bounty*. One may search in vain throughout logbooks, journals and diaries of the men of such ships, without finding any mention of a song or singing. Merchant Jack, however, did compose a shanty, somewhere around the turn of the century, telling of Bligh's voyage and the subsequent mutiny, but to keep the chronological record straight we will leave this until later.

From the ground we have covered so far, concerning the whole of the seventeenth and the greater part of the eighteenth centuries, various points become clear:

(1) so-called sea-songs were mainly the work of shore ballad-makers;

(2) a lesser number of genuine sea-songs, a few of which have come down to us, were made by sailors or pressed men;

(3) dramatists and composers of repute had their hand in the sea-songwriting pie;

(4) singing aboard naval ships at sea, while the wars with France, Spain and American Colonies were raging, was, generally speaking, looked upon as a sign of poor discipline;

(5) songs eulogising the naval sailor were plentiful, almost entirely overshadowing songs about merchantmen;

(6) merchant ships, being small with large crews,

   (a) had no need of a shanty to make up for the loss of ten men on a rope, or

   (b) had foreign crews without a true British sailor shantyman, who most probably would have been pressed and made to serve aboard a ship-of-the-line, with his shanties buried in his "chain-locker for the duration";

(7) shanties were taboo in the King's Service, and if they did exist among merchant seamen, were probably laying dormant for the time being, and therefore are patently absent from the sea literature of the period.

As Doerflinger[16] points out, it wasn't until the 1760s that British writers showed much interest in shore folk-songs. As for shanties, if they existed, well can we imagine them being by-passed by the so-called intelligentsia as bawdy songs, of poor construction musically, and quite beneath their contempt.

Before we pass on to shanties and Merchant Service forebitters, let us take a quick glance at the naval songs popular in Nelson's day and shortly after. Naturally, many were sung praising the great hero himself. One of these is even occasionally heard today in some folk-song clubs. This is *Lord Nelson's Victory at Copenhagen*.

Draw near ye gallant seamen, while I the truth unfold,
Of as gallant a naval victory as ever yet was told,
The second day of April last, upon the Baltic Main,
Parker, Nelson and their brave tars, fresh laurels there did gain.
With their thundering and roaring, rattling and roaring,
Thundering and roaring bombs.

Many songs relating to Trafalgar were produced by the broadside makers, of which the following was a favourite:

Come all ye British heroes, come listen to my song,
'Tis of a noble battle by our brave seamen won,
The twentieth of October that was the very day,
When the combined fleets from Cadiz, my boys, did put to sea.

Another, called *Nelson and Collingwood*, is given by Ashton.

Between 1815 and 1870, nautical songs issued by the printers were numerous. There were not so many martial ones as in earlier years, however; the tendency was towards Jack's amatory adventures ashore. It is rather interesting to note that, both from printed and oral sources, songs of the amorous adventures of the naval tar were rarely set against the background of the great naval ports of Portsmouth and Plymouth. I mean songs in which the pubs, whores and sleazy streets of the port concerned are named and described. I know of only one song relating to the nautical "nightside" of

[16] SHANTYMEN AND SHANTYBOYS (New York, 1951, p. 93).

31

Plymouth, and this was sung to the tune of the *Gendarmes' Duet*. It begins:

> Down the starboard side of Union Street,
> There dwelt a whore so young and fair . . .[17]

In fact, it would seem from the ballads that London was the only place in which the naval tar went on the "ran-tan", since Wapping and the Ratcliffe Highway have always been popular centres around which shoreside, amatory naval broadsides were built. Of course, there may be some confusion as to whether these Ratcliffe Highway ballads were really naval. The fact that such expressions as "frigate" and "stern-chasers" are included in them does not definitely point to a naval origin since merchant seamen from the early East Indiamen, which berthed in London, also used such terms as much as did men-o'-war's crews.

Here is a broadside song of latterday slave-chasing, printed by H. Such, of Union Street, London. It was extremely popular, both on the lower-deck and in the fo'c'sle, and I have a copy of it in my grandfather's handwritten songbook. This was one of the famous Henry Russel songs, the words by Angus B. Reach.

> Set every stitch of canvas, lads, to catch the flowing wind,
> Our bowsprit points to Cuba, an' the coast lies far behind;
> Fill to the hatches full, me boys, as o'er the sea we go,
> There's twice five hundred niggers down in the hold below.

Another late nineteenth-century song, a great favourite both with naval tars and Merchant Johns, is *Common Sailors*. My father often sang this, accompanying himself on a "squeeze-box".

> Now I'm a man before the mast, that ploughs this trackless sea,
> An' on this simple subject would you please enlighten me,
> Common sailors we are termed, tell me the reason why,
> That nasty, sneering adjective to our calling should apply.

Billy Boy is a shoreside ditty with a good "coal-box"—Jack's term for an all-hands-in chorus—which after becoming "salt-waterified" was also sung by both naval and merchant seamen:

> Will ye go to Cawsand Bay, Billy Boy, Billy Boy!

[17] We are not concerned, of course, with "modern" songs in this vein, of which there are many.

32

As is generally known nowadays, this song was sometimes used as a work-song, particularly in ships from the north-east coast. Although we have no proof that shanties did exist in the eighteenth century, nevertheless, it must be fairly obvious that the ones which have survived to the present day, and which were recorded in print during the first thirty years of the nineteenth century, must have been around for some time since they were set down, not as something new, but as a type of song already well established, and the art of shantying an already well-seasoned nautical custom.

Hauling songs such as *Boney*:

> Boney was a warrior,
> *Way, high, ya!*
> A warrior, a terrier,
> *John Franswar!*

and *Blood-red roses*:

> You bonny bunch o' roses O!
> *Hang down, ye blood-red roses!*

probably stem from ballads of the later period of the Napoleonic Wars, the phrase "blood-red roses" being a name given to the

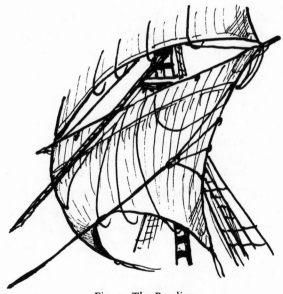

Fig. 5. The Bowline

English "redcoats" by Boney's men, or so it is said. From such slim clues, I feel we are right in saying that, although there is no real proof that shantying existed at all during the greater part of this period, from roughly 1780 until 1811, shanties in fact existed. The ones we have with us today were possibly created during these years. This is also, I feel, the period in which the greater number of salty forebitters were made. We are familiar with the theory that *A-rovin'* comes from a shore song of the seventeenth century—a catch in Thomas Heywood's play *The Rape of Lucrece* (1640)—but I have had the temerity to doubt this. Patterson writes that *Whiskey Johnny* was probably sung in Tudor times as *Malmsey Johnny*. This, too, is obviously a pleasant yarn without foundation. *Haul on the Bowline* has frequently been offered as a true hangover from the days of Henry VIII, on such technical grounds as that the bowline was only used to any effect aboard galleons, carracks and so on. But here again, although a bowline shanty did exist in the year 1493, the one given in the COMPLAYNT OF SCOTLAND:

> Hou, hou, pulpela, pulpela,
> Boulena, boulena,
> Darta, darta,
> Hard out strif.

is not *Haul the Bowline* as we know it. Incidentally, although the bowline became a rather negligible rope aboard merchantmen—the shanty *Haul the Bowline* being used solely on the sheets—the bowline was an important piece of cordage in the senior service, every squaresail having a pair, and this remained so until the last days of the "Sailing Navy". Some of the windlass and brake-pump shanties, however, ones such as *Lowlands*, *Sally Brown* and *Round the Capstan Go*, and hauling songs of the *Hanging Johnny* and *Cheerily Man* type, may quite possibly have been born in the late or mid-eighteenth century. *Sally Brown*, for example, was well known when Captain Marryat first referred to it[18] in 1837. In the quaint little volume called THE QUID[19] (page 222), two songs are given as having been sung aboard a certain East Indiaman in the 1830s. Doerflinger cites these as the first shanties in print. One is probably a shore-

[18] A DIARY IN AMERICA.
[19] London, 1832.

song roped in for the occasion—sailors often did this—and the other is a whaler's forebitter, used as a capstan song, which begins:

> Oh, her love is a sailor,
> His name Jemmy Taylor,
> He's gone in a whaler,
> To the Greenland Sea.

My friend G. Legman, on page 228 of his type-facsimile edition of Burn's MERRY MUSES OF CALEDONIA (New York, 1965), gives an unexpurgated version of this. It appears to have a fair age. In my own researches, I have come across two capstan songs (probably they were jack-screw shanties, of which more later) given in the book LANDSMAN HAY as having been sung by negro stevedores in Jamaica in the year 1811.

> Two sisters courted one man,
> *Ch.* Oh, huro, my boys,
> And they live in the mountains,
> *Ch.* Oh, huro boys O.
>
> Grog time of day, boys,
> Grog time of day,
> *Ch.* Huro, my jolly boys,
> Grog time of day.

Until recently, I too felt that these were, in all probability, the earliest printed shanties. Folk-song research workers and collectors have all striven hard to find a shanty in print in an eighteenth-century book, but still they haven't netted that will-o-the-wisp of Shantydom.

Perhaps what I have now to offer may be accepted as a captive for the net. Two or three years ago the well-known American marine historian Dr John Lyman lent me a copy of a rather rare collection of shanties, published in Denmark.[20] These shanties were collected by a certain Captain Oscar Jensen, and are given in both Danish and English. In addition to well-aired sea work-songs, there are several unusual shanties not to be found elsewhere. One of these, a pumping song called *Packet Ship*, may be the one and only shanty which, up to the present, we can place earlier than 1811, perhaps even in the 1790s.

[20] INTERNATIONALE SØMANDS-OPSANGE, 1923.

It is of the narrative type, with a semi-historical account of the mutiny of the *Bounty*. Strangely enough *Bounty's* captain is called "Blight", whether by accident or design we know not. Perhaps it was a suggestive tally given him by some shipboard wag. It starts:

> Bounty was a packet ship,
> *Ch.* Pump ship, packet ship!
> Cruising on a trading trip,
> *Ch.* In the South Pacific.

and goes on to relate the hardships of the men and their hazing by the tyrant "Blight". It is the final stanza, the eighteenth, however, that more or less places the age of the shanty:

> Never was there heard a word,
> From the crew that stayed on board.

As Captain Jensen in his notes points out, the mutiny took place in 1789, and until an American ship—a sealer—in 1809 discovered the mutineers on Pitcairn Island, the civilised world was ignorant of their fate. So, writes Captain Jenkins, since the last stanza declares the fate of the mutineers to be unknown, the date of the shanty must be placed before 1809. The book is dated 1923, but obviously Captain Jenkins collected his songs at sea at least twenty-five years earlier than the publication of the book, and since he writes that this

Fig. 6. "Thar she blows!"

shanty must be well over a hundred years old, this places it just inside the eighteenth century.

This is all we know of shanties made or used within the years 1780 and 1830. After this, the scope widens and material increases. With regard to forebitters, many of these must have been conceived during the latter years of the eighteenth century, their contents showing clues to their age. Whaling songs too, we can judge in this manner. One or two of those which tell of Greenland whaling, we can place most certainly in the eighteenth century. The songs of the South Seas sperm whalers are, in general, from around the turn of the century or perhaps a few years later. *The Whale* comes into the first category:

> And to Greenland cold sailed we, brave boys,
> And to Greenland cold sailed we.

with the following a good example of the South Seas whalemen's songs:

> 'Tis advertised in Boston, New York an' Buffalo,
> Five hundred brave Americans a-whalin' for to go . . .

In America, patriotic naval or semi-naval songs came into being during the latter part of the War of Independence: around 1879–1881. In the main, the few that exist follow the style of those in the Mother Country, eulogizing the naval sailor—although in America of those days, he was usually a merchant seaman or a landlubber serving aboard a merchant ship, tricked out naval fashion and probably called a privateer. One famous song coming from those days is, of course, *The Stately Southerner*, which can most likely be dated 1777. But like the sea-songs of England, those of America did not tell the true story of a sailor's life under the shipboard iron discipline and cruelties, with perhaps the exception of one song. This song, called *Captain James*, has come down to us thanks to whalemen's journals and to the fine research done by Gale Huntingdon in his recent book SONGS THE WHALEMEN SANG.[21] In this book, Huntingdon gives three versions—one possibly a broadside version—obtained from journals of the ship *Walter Scott*, the ship *Cortes* and the whaling brig *Two Brothers*. The journal of the latter

[21] Barre, Massachusetts, 1964.

bears the date 1768. In each version the unnamed ship, aboard which the cabin boy is ill-treated and eventually killed by the cruel master, was homeward-bound from Carolina or South Carolina. She was probably an inshore whaler. The boy in each song, however, bears a different surname—Richard Paddy, Richard Peve and Richard Spry—but in each case, the boy is mastheaded. Captain James, in all the versions, is hanged for killing the lad. The *Walter Scott* version has nineteen verses and appears to be more of a broadside than the other two. A British version, recorded by A. L. Lloyd, is called *The Cruel Ship's Captain*. The sleeve notes[22] say that a whaling captain (nameless) of King's Lynn, Norfolk, England, was hanged for the murder of the apprentice. However, this version has three verses only and Lloyd says that the long-winded ballad of the street singers was cut down by seamen, leaving what is "one of the briefest and most ferocious of sea-songs". The similarity between the songs of the two countries can be seen from certain couplets describing the lad in misery aloft, either at the masthead or on the frozen yard:

> With his hands and arms extended,
> I no succour to him gave
>
> (American version)

> When his eye and his cheek did hang towards me,
> With his hands and his feet bowed down likewise
>
> (English version)

Of course, I may be wrong in assuming that the versions from the whalemen's journals are of Colonial American origin—they may have come from England, the ship concerned being an English whaler. This is doubtful, however.

A long ballad, singing of slavery and piracy, which may have evolved during the first quarter of the nineteenth century, is known as *The Flying Cloud*. This may or may not be claimed by America, although I feel that Ireland is its most likely birthplace. Around that time, Acts of Congress had outlawed slavery in America and piracy

[22] *The Singing Sailor*—Workers' Music Association, London (12" LP). A fuller version of seven verses was recorded from the singing of Harry Cox of Norfolk. See JOURNAL OF THE ENGLISH FOLK DANCE AND SONG SOCIETY, Vol. VIII, No. 3 (Dec. 1958) under the title *The Captain's Apprentice*.

Fig. 7. Slaver

was being cleared from the Caribbean by the united efforts of American and European men-o'-war.

The American War of Independence (1812) produced a few patriotic and obviously shore-composed sea-songs, such as *The Constitution and the Guerriere* and *Ye Parliament of England*, but it is difficult to say whether they were popular with the seamen of the young nation.

We have touched upon British and American eighteenth- and nineteenth-century sailor songs singing of romantic love, gales, traditions, fights, slavery and piracy, death at sea and, in one or two cases, of cruelty on shipboard, but how about ones dealing with uninhibited sex and the price the sailor had to pay for such? This must have been a theme for nautical song-writers, or so many people would think—"you know what sailors are" being the thought running through their minds. In fact, although sex was obviously a factor of prime importance in the life of Jack ashore, and the resulting disease, a curse of the 'tween-decks and fo'c'sle, no one, so far as we know, voiced it in song—with one exception, and quite an old exception at that.

This exception was the famous old forebitter usually called *The Ratcliffe Highway*, sometimes *The Fireship*, and at times *The Blackballer*. It was popular both with the Johnny Haul-tauts of the Navy and with Merchant John. The theme, which is much the same in all versions and told in a nautical *double-entendre*, runs somewhat like this: A sailor ashore down Wapping way chases a "flash packet" and the two of them get drunk in a tavern. She then takes him to her "dive" and in the penultimate verses the sailor either gets robbed or "dosed", or both, the song finishing up with him either waking up aboard ship with a fat head or else in some early "Lock" hospital. Catnach published a broadside of this song in the first half of the nineteenth century, but the earliest version is that found in the PEPYS' BALLADS, dating from the war with the French, say about 1684. Here it is called *The Fireship*, a title often given to another sailor song sometimes called *The Dark and Rolling Eye* which is also of fair antiquity and with a similar theme since the sailor who chases the "fire-ship" eventually gets "burnt".

Fig. 8. Flash packet chase

By comparing the first couplets of some of the variants of *The Ratcliffe Highway* song, the reader will appreciate how usual a thing it was for a song to be twisted in the mouths of different singers.

Now as I was a-rollin' (cruisin') down Ratcliffe Highway,
A flash lookin' packet I chanct for to see.

Strolling through Norfolk one day on the spree,
I met a fair packet, her sails blowin' free.

An honest Jack Tar, oh, a-cruisin' did go,
And rollin' through Wapping, fell in with a beau.

As Jack walked one morning Point Beach up an' down,
He spied pretty Polly of merry Portsmouth town.

As Jack was a-rollin' round the Highway one morn,
He spied a flash packet of old Wapping town.

As I was a-cruisin' round Yarmouth one day . . .

As I was a-rollin' round London,
Through Wapping, 'long Ratcliffe Highway . . .

And here is a very modern version I picked up from "over the water":

I was sailing up Broadway one fine summer's day,
When a trim-lookin' craft I spied comin' my way;
I gave her a hail as she came alongside,
"I'm a Chinatown bum, going out with the tide."

As if the different sets of words are not enough to manage, each variant has a different, or slightly different, air. There is so much material and so many variants in relation to this song and its counterpart, *The Dark and Rolling Eye*, that I intend, at some later date, to write a study on this ancient and traditional sailor song.* A song with a similar tale, or rather a similar dismal ending to such an experience, is that called *A Young Sailor Cut Down in His Prime*, and this is still going strong in the folk clubs. Many versions of this song are to be found in which the dying or dead victim of a diseased harlot is a soldier or a cowboy. One typical case has the tragedy in reverse, since a female is the victim. Who was the first of these unfortunates we will never know, but the version in which a sailor is the "unfortunate rake" was certainly being sung in the early nineteenth century, if not in the latter days of the eighteenth century. Probably it is a toss-up between the soldier and the sailor as to which was the original victim, since both have been known to frequent the dens of such "ladies".

Having reached this type of sailor song, we can now consider the fo'c'sle song or forebitter, called by Americans "mainhatch

* See SPIN, Vol. 16, Nos. 3, 4, 5 and 6.

songs". Such songs were conceived somewhere between 1780 and 1830. These, along with the shanties, can be considered to be the only sailor-made songs. It is extremely noticeable that such landsman publishers as Catnach, Pitts, and Such of the "Seven Dials", London, and elsewhere their predecessors, the black-letter and white-letter ballad-makers and the chapbook and slipsong writers of the seventeenth and eighteenth centuries, put out songs of the type that sing of the sea, its ships, their rigging, of gales and wrecks, of sea-fights and whale-fights, female seamen, sea-cannibalism, and so on. On the other hand, those songs composed entirely by seamen generally have as their themes the shore delights of the ports. A sailor, no matter how much a dyed-in-the-hemp, tarry old seaconey he was, always turned his eyes shorewards towards the delights of Sailortown, as opposed to the land-bound sea-song composer who turned his to the rolling main, the balmy breezes, the thundering gales, the wet sheets and flowing seas, and the gallant barques manned by True Blues, Long John pirates, Cap'n Ahab whalemen and Will Watch smugglers. This, I'm afraid, appears to damn all sea-songs (we have no evidence of shanties) written before 1780 or thereabouts as being the work of longshore composers and therefore, in the main, telling of what the landlubber wanted the sailor to be, and not what out naval tars and Merchant Johns really were. This, I'm certain, is a fairly accurate statement: even the songs of whalers and pirates were rarely written or made up by the seamen concerned—the broadside makers did the job for them, although sometimes the sailors did trim and shorten the ballad-men's work to suit themselves. But when the forebitter proper made its appearance, along with the shanties we know today, a true picture was painted for the first time of, at least, Merchant John as he saw himself, and not as viewed through the eyes of the literary longshoreman.

Forebitters were sung for relaxation in the two-hour-long second dog-watch, the only actual leisure time a merchant seaman had at sea in sailing-ship days; work and sleep occupied all the remainder of the twenty-four hours. In port, the sailor worked, roughly, from 6 a.m. to 6 p.m., except when on anchor-watches. The sea-watches, from 8 p.m. one day until 4 p.m. the next, were of four hours' duration—four hours on and four hours off, or four hours' work and four hours' sleep—but the period from 4 p.m. till 8 p.m. was divided into two watches of two hours each. These were called dog-watches, from 4 to 6 p.m. being the first dog-watch, and from 6 to 8 p.m. the second dog-watch. During the first dog-watch, the sailor did some work and also ate, but the second dog-watch, apart from a little pulley-hauling, steering and lookout, was one of leisure. However, in dirty weather in the Western Ocean, as seamen called the North Atlantic, off the pitch o' the Horn and doubling the Cape of Good Hope, there was little opportunity for leisure of any kind. To the watches, normally on "standby" at such times, oilskin-clad and imprisoned in ropeyarn ties known as "soul and body lashings", awaiting the cry of "Aaall hands", singing and skylarking would be far from their minds. But in the steady warm trade winds, or even in the usually steady though strong "brave west wind" of the Roaring Forties, the second dog-watch would be a period of song and music.

In the tropics, when barely a rope would be touched, the hands would gather around the knightheads, under the cool down-draught of the fore-topmast-stays'l, with pipes going and chaws of baccy in their cheeks. Or maybe they would sit on the fore-bitts, close to the windlass or capstan, their bare feet dangling on the warm planking of the deck. Perhaps the ship would have a "fufu" band, consisting of a squeeze-box (concertina), a fiddle (very often home-made from a cigar-box), triangles, "spoons" and pig-bladder drums (the bladders having been extracted from the stores, by bribing a sea-cook). Running the Easting Down, the same scene would be enacted in the stuffy fo'c'sle, everything battened down to help keep the "fug" inside. The men would be seated on their sea-chests or, in later days, on benches with their elbows on the long tables, with the smoking oil-lamp swinging in its gimbals overhead, and the creaking timbers and eerie swish of oilskins hanging from their pegs forming background noises to the singing of these fine salt-water ditties.

Of course, it should not be thought that sailors sang nothing but sea-songs. Sailors, in fact, were quite catholic in their musical tastes. Shore love songs, drinking songs, popular music-hall ditties, pidgin-English snippets picked up in foreign parts (often garbled and entirely unintelligible to the natives of the countries from which they had been learned) and songs from the respective birthplaces of the men of many races who usually made up the "crowd" of a latterday windjammer, would all be voiced in the dog-watch. On the other hand, many shore-composed sea-songs had no place in fo'c'sle "banyans",[23] at least not in merchant ships of the nineteenth century. *Tom Bowling*, for example, was banned on superstitious grounds; it was considered a harbinger of death if sung, most certainly someone would fall from aloft or be killed in some strange way, or so sailors believed. As already stated pirate ballads, such as *Captain Kidd* with its endless verses and *High Barbaree*, were popular with the crowd. But the forebitter proper was something apart—a salty folk-song created by the seafolk. Many of these songs were of the type in which Sailor John gets robbed and bilked by shore-harpies. *Maggie May* and *Jack-all-alone* come into this category:

> When I ran into her, I hadn't got a care,
> I was cruisin' up an' down ol' Canning Place;
> She was dressed in a gown so fine, like a frigate of the line,
> An' I being a sailorman gave chase . . .
>
> *(Maggie May)*

> When I came to me senses, oh, nothin' could I find,
> But a woman's shirt an' apron there upon the bed did lie;
> I wrung me hands, I tore me hair, I yelled, "What shall I do ?"
> And said, "Farewell, O Wigan town, I'll never more see you."
>
> *(Jack-all-alone)*

Then there were those in which the sailor gained his objective to the discomfiture of his rivals; songs, such as *Cawsand Bay* (a variant of an older ballad *The Valiant Maid*) and *Doo Me Amma*, two always included in dog-watch concerts. Of course, many of these sailor-made songs would be forthrightly obscene or at least bawdy. *First Came the Bosun's Wife* is one I call to mind, and *Slack Away Yer Reefy Tackle* another.

Of the early forebitters, one good example from the late eighteenth century is *The Girls Around Cape Horn*:

> 'Tis the famed ship Garibaldi-O, a ship of high renown,
> There she lay, in Liverpool Bay, just close to old Liverpool
> town;
> Awaiting there for orders, boys, to take us far from home,
> Our orders came for Rio, boys, and then around Cape Horn.

[23] *Banyan*: This expression for a "party" probably harks back to the days of the East Indiamen. In India, in early times, religious festivals were held under the branches of the great banyan trees.

There were many versions of this, each having a ship of different name. Both naval and merchant-seamen versions exist, although I feel the naval versions with the name of a frigate are probably the older.

Outward and Homeward Bound is another forebitter of fair age, and here again some think it may have had naval origins, but most likely it was the work of some tarry mariner of the old East Indiamen.

> To the Blackwall Docks we'll bid adieu,
> To Sal and Kate and Bessie, too;
> The anchor's aweigh and our sails are unfurled,
> And we're bound to plough the watery world,
> Oh, say we're outward bound,
> Hurrah we're outward bound!

It was during the early days of the Western Ocean packets, however, that sailor-made forebitters really grew in numbers. With the cessation of the Napoleonic Wars in 1815 and the American War of Independence in 1812, merchant ships and seamen, as opposed to naval ships and seamen, began to come into the public eye. The ships developed in design, rigging and canvas, and Merchant John found a new freedom. No longer was he liable to be torn away from his ship, his home and his wife to serve for many years as a salt-water slave aboard one of the wooden walls of England. The piratical press-tenders were no longer needed and, thanks to the sailor being freer and naturally happier, forebitters and shanties grew in number. Heaving to the fiddle and fife and silent hauling to numbers and the bosun's pipe gave way to the singing of rousing capstan songs, boisterous hauling songs, and the wild falsetto sing-outs of hand-over-hand pulley-hauling. In fact, the great constructive period of the shanty is now agreed to have been between the 1820s and the 1850s, with many forebitters being born aboard the Western Ocean packets during the same period.

Following hard upon the heels of the Post Office "coffin brigs" and Falmouth packets—the first regular, if rather unseaworthy, "mail liners" to cross the North Atlantic, linking the new America with the Old Country—came the American-owned packet ships. Many thousands of under-nourished, impoverished, woebegone and forlorn emigrants from Ireland, Germany, Holland, Scandinavian and mid-European countries crossed the stormy Western

Fig. 9. Packet ship

Ocean. They travelled in the 'tween-decks of the packets of the Black Ball, Black Cross, Red Cross, Swallow Tail, and other mail lines, and had their first view of the fabulous New World from a shed in Castle Garden, New York:

'Twas at the Castle Garden, oh, they landed me ashore,
Heave away, me Johnnies, heave away, away!
An' if I marry a Yankee boy, I'll cross the seas no more,
Heave away, me bully boys, we're bound to go!

So runs this well-liked windlass shanty that came into being around the 1840s, the period of the Irish Potato Famine. At this time, Liverpool was the jumping-off place for the New World, and in this great port, around the Prince's Dock and the Pierhead, busy scenes of departure were daily occurrences. Forests of masts and yards met the eye at every turn, with topmen aloft loosing sails and leading down the gear prior to sailing. On the cluttered quayside the carters with their baggage drays, tarpaulin-hatted mariners smelling of tar, along with the ubiquitous ships' chandlers and beaver-hatted shipping agents, bustled to and fro jostling the lost-looking emigrants from the Ould Sod and mid-Europe. These latter would very often be sea-booted, be-kirtled and kerchiefed women with crying babies slung athwart their hips, the older children clinging to their mothers' voluminous skirts, with their bearded and fur-hatted, or clay-pipe smoking, knee-breeked better-halves standing guard over their miserable luggage.

The packets were, in the main, fairly fast sailors, but slowcoaches were plentiful too. From the numerous ships' chandlers, waiting like hawks for their victims, the emigrants had to buy their donkey's breakfasts (straw palliasses) and oatmeal, the staple food of packet-ship passengers. This meal could also be bought on board the ships. But, since many of the packets advertised themselves as mail boats (thereby suggesting speed), the emigrants, the Irish ones anyhow, got things a bit mixed. When unscrupulous agents informed them that some old slowcoach had a thousand bags of meal aboard —oatmeal, to an Irishman, was "oatmale"—they would join such a packet, believing they were boarding a fast ship carrying the mail. This is the theme around which the shanty *We're All Bound to Go* is woven:

Oh, yes I've got a packet ship, today she does set sail,
  Heave away etc,
With five and fifty emigrants and a thousand bags of "male",
  And away etc.

Most of the men who manned these Western Ocean packet ships were of Irish nationality—Irish from the Ould Sod, Liverpool Irish and New York Irish. They were known as Packet Rats and they were responsible for many fine forebitters, such as *The Liverpool Judies, Paddy Lay Back, Paddy West, The Banks of Newfoundland, The Liverpool Packet* and so on, many of which were used as capstan shanties. They were responsible too for the following windlass, halyard, pumping and sheet shanties: *Leave Her, Johnny, Leave Her* (first sung as *Across the Rocky Mountains* and *Across the Western Ocean*), *Blow the Man Down, The Blackball Line, Time for Us to Go* or *A Hundred Years Ago*, and many others. Some of these forebitters and shanties have airs reminiscent of those of Erin's Isle, and *Can't Ye Dance the Polka?* (which came into being around the 1840s when the polka spread from Bohemia all over the civilised world) unmistakably has the air of *Larry Doolan*, a well-known Irish song.

As well as being good shantymen and good shanty and forebitter makers, these Packet Rats were also excellent seamen, but (and

47

there is a "but") they were, to use a nautical expression, "hard men to shave". They probably were the toughest seamen salt water has ever known. And the afterguards of the packet ships, the captains and mates, had to be tough to handle them. The mates were named Blowers, Greasers and Strikers, and could throw a nifty right hook when the situation demanded it. Belayin'-pins were the favourite law enforcers, with the handspikes used in the capstan a second favourite. In fact, as the shanty has it, "belayin' soup an' handspike hash" was the daily routine aboard the packets. Some of these Packet Rats banded together under the name of the Bloody Forty in order to "trim the whiskers" of hardcase afterguards, and in many cases they were successful. However, when thirty of them signed under Captain Samuels in the *Dreadnaught*, the famous Wild Boat of the Atlantic, in order to perform this hirsute operation on the captain, they found they had picked the wrong man to deal with. Samuels, almost single-handed, turned the tables on them and decisively tamed the Bloody Forty.

Many of the emigrants from Europe who travelled in the damp and stinking 'tween-decks of the packets may have had a hand in the making of new shanties, or perhaps it would be truer to say that the Packet Rats heard the emigrants singing songs of their respective homelands—Scandinavian ballads, German hymns and Slavonic folk-songs—and from scraps of these turned out new salt-water ditties. Some authorities think that this may have taken place in the case of *Blow the Man Down*, since its first few bars have some similarity to the tune of the German carol *Stille Nacht, Heilige Nacht*.

Unfortunately, before the 1850s neither shanties nor forebitters were mentioned as such in the nautical literature of the day. The American writer Dana, in his TWO YEARS BEFORE THE MAST,[24] gives a list of shanties sung aboard the American ships *Pilgrim* and *Alert*, in which he served between the years 1834 and 1836 while engaged in the hide trade out in the small ports of what was then Spanish California. Here they are:

> *Heave to the Girls*
> *Cheerily Man*
> *Round the Corner*
> *Hurrah, Hurrah, My Hearty Fellows*

[24] New York, 1840.

48

Nancy O !
Captain's Gone Ashore
Heave Round Hearty
Jack Crosstree
Roll the Old Chariot
Neptune's Raging Fury

Elsewhere, he gives *Cheer Up Sam* (which is really a minstrel song) as a shanty that they used. But nowhere does he use the word "shanty". He calls them such things as "Songs for capstan and falls". Until Dr Lyman (in INTERNATIONALE SØMANDS-OPSANGE) found *The Packet Ship* (late eighteenth century), the present writer the two work songs in LANDSMAN HAY (1811), and Doerflinger the two songs in THE QUID (1832), Dana's was considered to be the earliest instance of shanties named in literature. Olmstead,[25] in his book about whaling in 1839–40, gives shanties with their tunes for the first time, but he does not call them shanties. The two he gives are *Drunken Sailor* and *Nancy Fanana*. He also mentions one used for pulling the teeth out of the jaw of a sperm whale, *O Hurrah, My Hearties O !*—which may be the same as Dana's *Hurrah, Hurrah, My Hearty Fellows*. THE QUID also refers to another work-song, *Pull Away Now, My Nancy O !*, which perhaps is the one listed by Dana as *Nancy O !*

A further development of the shanty occurred along with· the growth of the cotton trade between the Gulf ports of America and those of the Old World such as Liverpool, London and Le Havre. This trade started about the 1790s, when the invention of the cotton-gin in England brought about a demand for Southern States cotton. By 1837, the trade was in full swing[26] and the wooden droghers from Britain and elsewhere lay in their hundreds loading the bales alongside the river wharves of New Orleans, Mobile, Savannah and other Gulf ports. Now, the Packet Rats considered themselves deep-water sailormen only; dock labourer's work, that is working beside a ship in port, was to them anathema. So as soon as the packet moored in New York or Boston, many of them evolved a regular pattern of jumping the ship and heading south as fast as

[25] INCIDENTS OF A WHALING VOYAGE (New York, 1841).
[26] L. G. Carr Laughton, "Shantying and Shanties", THE MARINERS MIRROR, IX (1923).

their legs or a coast-wise vessel would take them. Others would leave their packets in order to dodge the hauling of frozen ropes and the wading waist deep in icy water at the lee fore brace during the W.N.A. (Winter North Atlantic), preferring the warmer climes of Louisiana until the spring came. In the Gulf ports, they would find plentiful employment as "hoosiers" or cotton stevedores, on the wharves and down the holds of the cotton ships. This stowing of the cotton bales in the holds of the wooden droghers was a most arduous task, originally undertaken by Negroes and Creoles, but from the 1830s and throughout the 1840s, white sailors took a big hand in "screwing cotton" as the job was called. In those days, they worked shoulder to shoulder with the coloured hoosiers, although in later years a system developed whereby Whites worked one hatch and Black another. This "screwing cotton" meant forcing the great bales into the dark recesses of the holds of the ships by means of jackscrews. The Negroes sang chants very similar in form to the sailor shanty as they hove around these great jackscrews. They would sing purely Negro work-songs as well as adapted songs that had come down from the interior by way of the great rivers (the Ohio, Missouri and Mississippi), songs of the river boatmen and early *voyageurs*. *Shenandoah*, once sung by the "Long Knives", cavalrymen, frontiersmen and mountain men, probably took this route to the wharves of Mobile and New Orleans. The white sailor-men, when they had had their bellyful of this arduous work— Nordhoff[27] calls it "the most exhausting labour that is done on shipboard"—returned to their normal occupation by joining cotton droghers bound for Europe.

Incidentally, it was quite feasible that many such seamen never reached port again, for these ships, justifiably called "coffin ships", often foundered in deep water. This was in the days before Samuel Plimsoll and his famous loading line. Cotton, if it becomes damp, swells a great deal, and for this to happen to the bales, already jammed to their utmost capacity by the great jackscrews, was extremely serious. These wooden ships would virtually come apart at their seams and founder in the middle of the Atlantic, miles from port, all hands going to Davy Jones' Locker, leaving only the owners (who would draw the insurance) to benefit from such losses. It is fairly obvious that when the packet seamen who worked on the

[27] THE MERCHANT VESSEL (Cincinatti, 1874).

wharves of the Gulf ports put to sea again, they would take with them new work-songs learned from the coloured cotton hoosiers, and they in their turn would bring new, Irish-shaped shanties to the Gulf for the coloured hoosiers to pick up. Hence these cotton ports could be called Shanty Marts, the exchange bureaux of the work-song. Nordhoff, writing of these white hoosiers in the 1840s, gives four "cotton chants" popular with the gangs. Two are unknown to us, never having left the Gulf to our knowledge; although the word "maringo" in the second one points to a possible Irish origin.

> Oh, we work for the Yankee dollar,
> *Ch. Hurrah, see-man, do!*
> Yankee dollar, bully dollar,
> *Ch. Hurrah, see-man, dollar!*

and
> Lift him up and carry him along,
> *Ch. Fire, maringo, fire away,*
> Put him down where he belongs,
> *Ch. Fire, maringo, fire away.*

As in deep-water shantying, a shantyman—and he was called just that—sang the solo lines, and on a certain word in the refrain (usually the last), the hoosiers would heave on the jackscrews forcing the bales more tightly into the dark, dark recesses of a ship's hold, even to the extent (as Nordhoff tells us) that "the ship's decks are raised off the stanchions which support them". Although Nordhoff uses the word "chantyman" for the leader of the gangs—the first time in print as far as we know—he does not use the words chanty or shanty. Probably the first man to print the word chanty is G. E. Clark, who also has "chanty-man" and "chanty-gang" many times in his book which was printed in 1867.[28] This latter term was an alternative name for the hoosiers. The other two chants which Nordhoff gives became well known all over the seven seas. The first of these is a *Stormalong* number (the mythical Old Stormy had many shanties built around him) and the second, *Highland Laddie*, was used both at sea, as a "walkaway" or "stamp 'n' go" song, and on the wharves of the world as a cargo-working song. Of course, this song had its origin in Bonnie Scotland, but, after being used as a

---

[28] SEVEN YEARS OF A SAILOR'S LIFE (Boston).

cotton stower's jackscrew chant, it soon became equally popular among the timber droghers of Quebec, Miramichi and elsewhere. The vessels engaged in the timber trade had square bow-ports, through which the huge bulks of timber could be launched into the

Fig. 10. Launching timber

holds. Tackles were rigged at salient points so as to handle the logs, and the falls of these would be led to deck capstans, around which the men, both stevedores and sailors, would tramp, vociferously singing *Highland Laddie* or one of its variants, such as *Donkey Riding* or *A Young Thing Lately Left Her Mammy O*. The Quebec timber-stowers in particular were a rough lot, and when, with winter approaching, the season drew to a close in their home port, they would head south either to work on the cotton wharves of the Gulf or to work at stowing hard pine in Doboy Sound. In later years when "daylight was let into the neck o' the woods" around Georgia and the pine depleted, they shifted to Florida, to the ports of Pensacola, Appalachicola, Pascagoula and so on, and loaded the "Quebec Fleet" there as well. As a result of this, one of the world's toughest sailortowns grew up around Lower Palafox Street, Pensacola, a sailortown inhabited and frequented by a knifing, eye-gouging, kicking and rum-swilling bunch of French-Canadian and Irish timbermen. A shanty, probably of Negro origin, popular with these pitch-pine gangs was *Way Down in Florida*:

> 'Way down South where the cocks do crow,
> *'Way down in Florida!*

Before we leave the cotton-stowers I would like to point out that, thanks to the Irish seamen bringing in fresh chants to the Gulf and picking up Negro songs from the hoosiers, many Irish/Negro shanties came into being about this time—such shanties as *Clear the Track and Let the Bulgine Run* and *Johnny Come Down to Hilo*, both of which have Irish airs and Negro words. In fact, *Clear the Track* has the tune of *Shule Agra*, a well-known Irish song.

A spate of new shanties evolved during the Sacramento gold-rush of 1848–49. In 1848, a man called Marshall, who worked at a sawmill called Sutter's Mill, on the banks of Sutter's Creek (a small tributary of the Sacramento River, California), discovered gold in its shallow and stony pools, and the world became gold mad.

In every shipyard around the eastern American seaboard, from Maine to Maryland, in every creek and tidewater, adzes and caulking mallets resounded through the pine forests. Every jobbing carpenter called himself a shipwright, and farmers left their homesteads to become dockyard workers. Some of the ships produced were the finest the world has ever seen, but many were "tubs" and "coffins". From Down-east ports the "fliers" glided down to the Line, thundered around the Horn, and belted their way up to this coast which, until now, had known only the stench of the whaleships and hide-droghers. And the slowcoaches and "wrecks" fumbled their way over the same route, many foundering off the Horn. Those that made the grade were beached on the sands of Frisco Bay, where they became prisons, hotels, chapels and brothels. Alternative routes to the diggings were by "prairie schooner" through Indian country, by the new-fangled steamboat from east-coast ports, or from New Orleans to Panama. After landing there, on what was then a wild Central American shore, the emigrants had to go on burro or on foot across the Isthmus of Darien, following much the same route as the Panama Canal was to follow. On

53

the Pacific shore—if they made it in spite of Chagres Indians, fever and famine—they would hopefully await the arrival of a ship to help them finish their argosy. Naturally, such a trek inspired a wealth of songs, although most of them were from the miner's and not from the sailor's point of view. Some overlapped, such as *Coming Round the Horn*:[29]

Now miners, if you'll listen, I'll spin ye quite a tale,
About a voyage around Cape Horn, they call a pleasant sail;
We bought a ship and had her stowed with houses, tools and
grub,
But cursed the day we ever sailed in that worn-out rotten tub.

Ch. Oh, I remember well, the lies they used to tell,
Of the gold so bright, it hurt the sight, and made the
miners yell.

After singing about the grub, the weather and the rounding of the Horn, an interesting verse tells of them putting into Valparaiso "Where the women are so loose", and how all the crew and the miners went ashore on the ran-tan. This song is one of the many put together by Old Put, a miner named John A. Stone, who made a small fortune at the diggings and set up a thriving song-making business.

Another of these semi-sea-songs was sung to the tune of *Pop Goes the Weasel*. In fact, most of the songs the miners sang adopted tunes from older songs. *Coming Round the Horn*, for example, was sung to the minstrel tune *Dearest Mac!* The new *Pop Goes the Weasel* ditty was christened *A Ripping Passage*. It was about a shipload of gold-seekers leaving New Orleans for Panama and their trials and tribulations are well aired. The verse that follows mentions the railroad and this dates the song a little later than most of these gold-rush ditties, since the forty-seven miles of crude railway was not built until a few years after the original rush. Sailors who had to use this Heath Robinson contraption used to call it "Going round the Horn in a railway carriage", since it saved them the rigours of rounding Cape Horn from the Atlantic to the Pacific.

[29] J. Monaghan, THE BOOK OF THE AMERICAN WEST (J. Messner, Inc., New York, 1963).

The cholera begins to rage and some have got the scurvy,
Chickens dying from old age, steerage arsey-turvey,
When ye git to Panama, greasers want a back-load,
Officers begin to jaw, rig goes the railroad!

A song with a similar theme, given in SONGS OF THE GOLDRUSH,[30]
is called *The Fools of '49*:

The poor, the old, the rotten scows,
Were advertised to sail,
From New Orleans with passengers,
But they must pump and bail.

Another ditty, popular with both sailors and miners, had this
chorus:

Jump away, Jonathan, jig along, Jemina,
Californy's made of gold, we'll all git rich as Lima;
Come lads, leave yer dads, to search for gold be brisk-O,
Cut stick, right quick an' sail for San Francisco!

According to Basil Lubbock,[31] a song every boy and girl was
singing and whistling around the New York waterfront area in the
1850s was:

I asked a maiden by my side, who sighed and looked to me
                                                    forlorn,
"Where was her heart?" she quick replied, "Round Cape
                                                    Horn!"

But one of the most popular of the earlier songs, one that was
even sung at the capstan-head aboard the good ship *La Grange* when
she sailed from Salem for Frisco in 1849—according to O. T. Howe,
in his ARGONAUTS OF '49 and one in which sailors and gold-seekers
alike bellowed the chorus, was *Californi-O!* It is said that it was
introduced (and written, I believe) by the Hutchinsons, a well-
known concert and minstrel troupe.

[30] Ed. by R. A. Durger and R. E. Lingefelter (Cambridge University Press,
England, 1965).
[31] THE DOWN EASTERS (Glasgow).

When formed our band, we are all well-manned,
To journey afar to the promised land;
The golden ore is rich in store,
On the banks of the Sacramento shore.

Ch. Then ho, boys, ho!
To California go!
There's plenty of gold in the world I'm told,
On the banks of the Sacramento shore.

About the same time, a capstan shanty called *Sacramento*—either
a sailor-made original or a variant of this song, it is difficult to say
—was being circulated among the crews of the Cape Horners bound
for California. To make matters more difficult for the student,
Stephen Foster, the American composer of *Jeannie With the Light
Brown Hair*, *Swannee River* and so on, copyrighted his *Camptown Races*
somewhere around this time. This had a "hoodah" refrain exactly
the same as that of the capstan shanty. Foster, however, did not
publish his song until 1856, by which time the shanty was well aired,
so it is difficult to know who stole from whom, or which came first.
C. Fox Smith[32] obtained from a certain Capt. J. L. Vivian Millet a
partly remembered gold-rush shanty which he once heard sung
aboard a ship weighing anchor in Algoa Bay. The chorus runs:

Goodbye, my love, goodbye,
No one can tell me why;
I'm bound to California,
To reap the shining gold.

We know that *O Susanna* was popular with the miners, but the sailors
also had a version, now unfortunately lost, except for two verses
collected by Miss Colcord:[33]

Holystone the cabin, boys, and git down on yer knees,
None of yer Limejuice touches,
In the *Sovereign of the Seas*.

Ch. O Susanna, darling take yer ease,
For we have beat the clipper fleet,
The *Sovereign of the Seas*.

---

[32] A BOOK OF SHANTIES (London, 1927).
[33] SONGS OF AMERICAN SAILORMEN (New York, 1938).

Fig. 11. A Cape Horner

Obviously this was sung about a smart clipper and not about one of the "slowcoaches".

As Doerflinger points out, the sailors of the sail took couplets and phrases from the songs of the so-called Nigger Minstrels, from those sung on the low stages of the melodeons and concert saloons of New York, Boston and New Orleans, ditties from the mouths of such characters as Gumbo Chaff and Pompey Smash, as well as from the throats of similar types who graced the music-hall stages of the seaports of Britain. Shanties like *A Long Time Ago* and *Do My Johnny Boker* obviously had such origins, as well as lines such as:

> Where there ain't no snow, and the winds don't blow
> We dug his grave with a silver spade,
> His shroud of finest silk was made

found in many shanties, e.g. *Santiana* and *Stormalong*.

There were many cheap songbooks published in the first half of the nineteenth century—ETHIOPIAN, NEGRO, NIGGER and CALIFORNIA SONGSTERS and NIGGER MELODIES—and these doubtless found their way into the voluminous pockets of mariners' peajackets. It is plain to see that songs from such books were the origin of some of the sailor shanties. There is one more source from which Sailor John purloined ideas for his work-songs, that of the railroad gangs of the New America. The brake-pump song *Paddy Works on the Railway* is one of these, although Terry[34] seems to think the tune, at least, comes from an older pederastically inclined shanty, *The Shaver*.

Let us now leave the New World and return to see how Britain was getting on during the first half of the nineteenth century.

The end of the famous East India Company's fleet, whose inception harks back to the time of Elizabeth I, came in 1834 when its "tea-wagons" were broken up or sold. In 1824, two partners, Money Wigram and Richard Green, started a Far Eastern line of sailing ships, but the partners later quarrelled, dividing the fleet between them. Wigram's flag is still with us today at the mastheads of the ships of the Federal line, but Green's flag is no longer flying, except on the caissons of the Blackwall Yard, London. Green ships, however, became world famous under the name of "The Black-wallers" or "Blackwall Frigates". Aboard these ships, or at least the earlier ones, built on the "cod's head, mackerel tail" principle, having enormous crews and heavily rigged, semi-naval or old John Company discipline prevailed for many years. Shantying was most likely prohibited. The fiddle was still the "musick" to which the seamen pranced around the capstan. C. Fox Smith believes, rightly so, that many shanty airs came from scraps of such fiddle tunes constantly ringing in the ears of the "Flying Fish Sailors", as the crews of the Blackwall frigates and their successors the tea clippers were nicknamed.

From the 1860s onwards, we have Captain Whall's[35] authority for it that shantying *was* the custom aboard these Blackwallers. Whall sailed in Green's ships from 1861 until their demise, which came about shortly after the opening of the Suez Canal, in 1869. He collected most of his shanties and sea-songs aboard these splendid passenger-carrying East Indiamen.

The fast Yankee clippers out to China started with the *Rainbow*,

[34] THE SHANTY BOOK (London, 1921–26).
[35] SEA SONGS AND SHANTIES (Glasgow, 1927).

launched in 1845. This was two years after the Treaty of Nanking and the opening of the ports. British clippers didn't get in the trade until about six years later, although the Blackwall frigates were bringing home tea during these years. It wasn't, however, until 1860—the Americans finished competing in 1859—that British tea clippers really filled the scene. Strangely enough, we do not know of any shanty being conceived aboard the clippers, in fact, since they often carried double crews when racing, it seems highly doubtful whether shanties were sung at all in these smart ships and certainly no reference is made to such singing in the contemporary literature of the tea clippers.

Gold was found in Australia in 1851–53, but until an agricultural peace fell on that up-to-then wild country of convicts and bushrangers, no regular shipping companies supplied the needs of the people of the "Colonies" as sailors called Australia. The ships of Green and Dunbar, however, made occasional passages out to Sydney in between Oriental voyages. With the opening of the Suez Canal in 1869 and the new-fangled "tin-kettles" taking over the China tea trade, many of the clippers and the newly found Baines' Blackball line began to carve regular trade routes between the Mother Country and the Colonies. Apart from the capstan shanty *South Australia*, no new work-songs were produced in these ships either, and many authorities feel that even this song, more than likely, started life in the days of the California gold rush, since versions are to be found giving:

> Heave away, haul away!
> And we're bound for California!

This brings us up to the late 1860s and early 70s, and on this note, let us return to the New World, this time to the West Indies. Bullen[36] was probably the first man to recognise the amount of West Indian influence in many shanties. Later, Terry concurred, while the present writer, who spent some time in the West Indies many years ago, came across several "new" shanties confirming this influence.

Since the days of the buccaneers, West Indians have served aboard British ships, both naval and merchant. By the early nineteenth century, the system known as "chequerboard watches" had become a

[36] SONGS OF SEA LABOUR (London, 1914).

59

recognised custom, particularly aboard the sugar-droghers out of Liverpool, Glasgow and Bristol. To explain this, it must be understood that aboard all ships in the old days the men were divided into two watches (nowadays, ships have three watches): the port and starboard. In the chequerboard system, if one starboard watch was made up of white seamen, the port watch would consist of black seamen, and I must say, with modern colour problems in mind, they got on very well together indeed.

It is well known that the shanties or clinker-built huts of the West Indian poorer classes, and in particular those of the fishermen, are built on piles for various reasons. One reason was so that shallow tin plates filled with turpentine or some other repellant could be placed on the top of the posts in order to prevent giant ants, land-crabs, snakes and scorpions from invading the house. Another reason was so as to make a space beneath the hut, in which domestic birds and animals could be housed in pens or tethered to the piles. From the point of view of our subject, however, the most important reason was the ease with which a shanty could be moved from one point to another when its occupants wanted a change of locale. This was often the case with fishermen's huts sited close to the beach. When a hurricane or tidal-wave threatened, they would move their huts further inland. Rollers would be inserted under the huts, the piles removed, and a whole village would be rolled away to a new site. Several families would participate in such a manœuvre, with every man, woman and child hauling away on the long warps fastened to each shack. On the roofs of the shanties a chant-leader or "header" would sit athwart the ridge, bawling out solo lines

Fig. 12. Moving house in the West Indies

with, as in the shanty, the gang coming in on the refrains. Another similarity to shantying was that on certain words in the refrains all hands would haul mightily. Except that it wasn't done aboard a ship's deck, this was, of course, shantying—real shantying.

But then again, many of these chants—as in the case of those of the hoosiers of Mobile Bay—were taken to sea by the Islanders. Going to sea in foreign-going sailing ships was one of the major occupations of the menfolk of the West Indies. And, naturally, many of these West Indian shanties were taken over by the white seamen—*Sally Brown* being a good example. Many were sung only by the black watch; the white watch probably found them too "sticky" for the average sailor singer. These shanties were usually hauling songs and, of the ones I collected from a wonderful West Indian shantyman called Harding the Barbadian Barbarian, the following were used at halyards aboard British and American square-riggers:

Ooh! Haul away for the windy weather, boys,
Haul away, boys haul away!
Ooh, Haul away an' pull tergether, boys,
Haul away, boys, haul away!

Oh, where am I to go me Johnnies, oh, where am I to go?
To me way, hay, hay, high, roll an' go!
For I'm a young sailor-boy, an' where am I to go?
To me way, hay, hay, high, roll an' go!

Ol' Cap'n Baker, how do yer stow yer carger?
Roll, boys, roll, boys, roll!
Some I stow for'ard, boys, an' some I stow after,
Way, high, Miss Sally Brown!

These are only a few from my collection. Frederick Pease Harlow gives several West Indian hauling songs in his book,[37] collected mainly from Barbados. The following three are from his collection:

> Come smilin' Lindy Lowe,
> De pootiest gal I know,
> *On de finest boat dat ever float*
> *In de Ohio,*
> *De Mississippi or de Ohio.*

> (*'Badian Hand-over-hand*)

[37] CHANTEYING ABOARD AMERICAN SHIPS (Barre, Massachusetts, 1962) pp. 201, 199, 85.

Every Sunday mornin',
John, John Crow,
When I go a-courtin',
John, John Crow.

(*Barbadian cargo shanty*)

Six o'clock I hear 'em say,
Sun down, sun down below,
Aye-a a-a-a
Sun down, sun down below.

(*West Indian cargo-working shanty*)

Over to the west'ard of the Islands lies a coastline that was well known to sixteenth-century sailors. Around Campeché in southern Mexico, and Belize in British Honduras, logwood and mahogany cutters, with crews often consisting of runaway sailors, have worked down through the centuries. Ships of all nations have frequented the bays and lagoons of this coast, loading the logwood and, as the lumbermen launched the logs through the bowports of the droghers, many a good shanty was sung. Many of these songs were picked up from the shore workers, songs of Afro-American and Latin mixture. The great majority of these have been lost, but the following is one which has survived:

Haul away for Campeachy Bay,
Dance, gals, gimme de banjo!
Oh, haul away, an' stretch out for yer pay,
Dance, gals, gimme de banjo!

And the Danish sailor-author Rasmussen gives us two more in his book;[38] one, a lumber-stowing shanty:

A de hala hombre poquito mas,
Dow below for rolling go!

the other, used for freeing logs in a 'jam':

Chyrra me Yankee, chyrra me rao,
What's de matta de loggin' no go ?

[38] SEA FEVER.

Over to the south-east lies the island of Trinidad and the Guianas. Shantymen from these romantic places also produced shanties:

Essequibo River is the Queen of rivers all,
Buddy tanna na, we are somebody O!
Somebody O, Johnny, somebody O,
Buddy tanna na, we are somebody O!

In the last century many of "Jimmy" Nourse's sailing ships, vessels with "river" names, left Liverpool with general cargoes for India. In such ports as Calcutta, Indian families were stowed in the 'tween-decks and carried as indentured labour to Trinidad and Demarara. The ships would finish the "triangle course" by taking rum and sugar back home. These ships all carried Lascar crews, and we do know that shanties, with texts in a bilingual Anglo-Hindi *bat*, were sung by these fine seamen, but apart from the following which I collected in Trinidad, I doubt if any have survived:

Ke, ke, ke, ke, *Ekidumah*!
Somerset a-killa coolie man, *Ekidumah*!
Somerset a-killa wire fall, *Ekidumah*!
Somerset a-killa bosun's mate, *Ekidumah*!

Probably the last really salty shanties to be produced were those coming from the saltpetre trade of the west coast of South America. Although this trade, along with that of copper-ore, in some small way, started around the last quarter of the eighteenth century, it wasn't until the last quarter of the nineteenth century that it reached its peak. In the 1870s, 1880s and 1890s, every port up and down the "Flaming Coast" of Chile had its quota of ships, moored in tiers, awaiting saltpetre cargoes from the mines inland. When the filthy cargo was loaded the men would be given a "sub" of money and one day's liberty. Then, once they had become loaded to the scuppers with *pisco* and *aquadiente*, all hell would be let loose and fighting, singing, prostitute-hunting gangs would roll around the sandy plazas "astonishing the natives". These were the seamen who turned out what was probably the most bawdy of all the songs of Shantydom. This, and not the fact that they were sung in rare trades as some "authorities" declare, is the reason why such latterday shanties rarely found their way into printed collections. The only collector I know who made any effort to put a few in print—camouflaged, as he himself admits—was the late Captain Robinson, who wrote several articles on shantying in a journal called THE BELLMAN[39] now out of circulation. From Liverpool seamen who once shipped in nitrate or saltpetre ships I obtained a few shanties, and these, naturally, I have had to camouflage. A great favourite was *Serafina*:

> The sailors when they leave the port are quite a few pounds
> leaner,
> *Serafina, Serafina!*
> It's not because they're short o' grub, it's because of Serafina,
> *Serafina, oh, Serafina!*

Two others are *The Gals of Chile* and the *Saltpetre Shanty*. The refrains of such shanties were originally odds and ends of Spanish phrases heard by the seamen ashore or from the Chileno *lancheros*. They wouldn't use these however, oh no! If some bawdy or obscene English word or phrase sounded anything like these pidgin-Spanish phrases, then these were the ones they included in the shanty refrains.

Troops have been carried by sailing vessels from the earliest times, and they were expected to haul and heave along with the sailors. The wars of the Napoleonic period, as already mentioned, produced the expression "blood-red roses", a name for the red coated British soldier. Some folk-club members seem to believe that the refrain of the halyard shanty, "Come down [or Go down], ye blood-red roses!" was a warning to the troops from the shanty-man to get out of the way when the sailors were working ship. Actually the reverse is more likely, and this is why I prefer the version of the refrain which runs, "Hang down, ye blood-red roses!" In other words, the shantyman included the "leathernecks" in his call to "bust the slings o' the Yard!" It may be that "Hang down, ye bloody roses [or posies]!" was what he really yelled.

At the time of the Crimean War and Indian Mutiny, naval steam frigates, as well as hired mail steamers, were used as troopships. H.M.S. *Malabar* and her four sisters the *Crocodile, Jumna, Euphrates* and *Serapis* of the 1860s, 1870s and 1880s were the first naval steam frigates to be built for the sole purpose of troop-carrying. Aboard these famous "lobster pots", the seamen did the work aloft while the soldiers were made to do the "pulley-hauley" work on deck.

[39] "Songs of the chantey-man", THE BELLMAN (Minneapolis, 14 July–4 Aug. 1917).

Their commands were given military fashion: "Quick march!" for "heave!" So writes R. A. Ramsdale,[40] on the authority of Admiral Lewis, who served in H.M.S. *Serapis*. These ships are often mentioned in the writings of Rudyard Kipling.

Fig. 13. A lobster pot

The wars of the nineteenth and twentieth centuries also had some bearing on shanties. From the marching songs of the American Civil War, both of the North and of the South, the sailor took the liveliest for use when marching around the capstan. His favourite was *John Brown's Body*, but he also sang *Maryland*, *The Yellow Rose of Texas*, and *Dixie* with equal gusto. A most popular true shanty also came from out of this war; this was *The Alabama*:

When the Alabama's keel was laid,
Roll, Alabama, roll!
They laid her keel in Birkenhead,
Roll, Alabama, roll!

The Crimean War of 1854–56 gave the seaman *Sebastopol* or *Cheer, Boys, Cheer!* and from the Boer War, or it may have been from the Zulu War, the shantyman got what was probably his last shanty, *We Are Marching to Pretoria*. This song was taken up by naval matlows during World War II and given many bawdy stanzas. And with this

[40] "Sea Breezes" (May, 1955) from a letter in the SLOP CHEST.

twentieth-century offering we may as well clew up our potted history of the working songs, as well as the songs of leisure, sung by the old tarry, brine-encrusted, sailing-ship mariners of the days that have gone.

HOW SHANTIES AND OTHER KINDS OF
SHIPBOARD SONGS WERE USED

*The 'Machinery' associated with them; Style of Singing;
Longshore Work-songs; etc.*

The first piece of ship's furniture with which a crowd of new
hands would come to grips on joining a fresh ship was the capstan.

Fig. 14. Capstan on the fo'c'slehead

In later sailing-ship days, this device was situated in the centre of
the fo'c'slehead, i.e. the raised section at the front end of the ship.
On the sailing day, the men—some the scrapings of the gutters of
the ports, others real deepwatermen who, however much they cursed
their trade, followed it faithfully to the end—would tumble out of
their bunks at the mate's roar "Aaaall hands!" With fat heads and
unsteady feet, they would stumble up the ladders leading to the
fo'c'slehead. Here they would gather, woebegone, beside the capstan, a fetish around which they would have to traipse many times
before the voyage was over in penance for having signed. On the
word of command, the handspikes would be shipped in the scarlet
pigeon-holes, the bars would be "breasted", and with shuffling gait
the men would commence the long "walk 'n' heave" around the
trundlehead. It is from this latter term that our shoreside word
"trundle" is derived.

Until this moment, the mate would be in total ignorance as to the

67

Fig. 15. Capstan bar

seamanlike qualities of the "crowd". Seeing that they had been brought aboard by the boarding-house masters the evening before —most, if not all, in various stages of drunkenness—for all he knew the whole raff might be nothing more than shanghaied yokels with hayseeds in their ears, or crimped counter-jumpers, pen-pushers and boot-blacks, or just plain, unwashed Sailortown derelicts.

Looking up from his sidelong inspection of the dripping links of the anchor chain as one by one they slowly emerge from the muddy surface of the water, the mate, clapping his hands to his mouth and with a roar like the Bull of Basham, queries, "Who's the bloody nightingale among yer? Aw ye men or aw ye cawpses? If there's a ruddy shantyman among yer lot of hobos, fer Gawd's sake strike a light, will yer!"

In answer to this challenge, from the cavernous throat of some true son of Neptune comes the hurricane reply:

"Oh, say wuz ye niver darn Ri-i-o Grande?"

The refrain, a bit seedy at first, comes from half of the heaving men:

"Wa-a-ay darn Ri-O!"

The self-imposed shantyman now really gets into his stride:

"Ooh! Them smart señoritas, they sure beats the band!"

And the sailormen, taking heart, bring in a fuller and beefier refrain:

"For we're barnd for the Ri-i-o Grande!"

A satisfied smile crosses the lips of the mate. He's got a good crowd; the shanty tells him that. "When the men sing right, the ship goes right" was the old sea adage.

Of course, there may be a suspicious feeling in the mind of the reader that sailors were some sort of singing puppets aboard a floating music-hall. This, however, was far from true. Shanties were sung at special jobs. They were "dedicated" to special jobs, and were not, for example, sung during shipboard leisure, nor ashore when, full of ale, the merry mariners would be lifting the rafters of some dockside tavern with their raucous voices. Since shanties were only sung when heaving at the capstan or hauling on cordage, and since sailors were not always engaged in such operations, there were many long periods—sometimes weeks and even months—when a capstan would not be turned, nor a rope started from its pin and, it follows, not a shanty of any kind raised. Sometimes, too, voyages were not very happy ones. Some were dark, blood-boat passages during which the sound of a song was never heard. And sometimes, on account of the rather bawdy nature of most shanties, there were religiously inclined masters who forebade the singing of them *in toto*.

The Windlass Shanty

The earliest form of capstan—in older books it is written "capstern" —was that known as a windlass, or windlash. Prior to this, in Biblical, Roman and Viking times, the seamen would haul directly on the cable. The windlass had a horizontal oak barrel or drum, the axle of which was set into two upright baulks of stout oak, bolted firmly to the deck. The anchor cable, usually of plaited rope (although in early times it was sometimes a sort of chain made from both iron and bronze with figure-of-eight links), was given several turns around this barrel. The whole apparatus was hove round by the seamen pulling on handspikes inserted in drums fitted on the same axle, but outside of the uprights or bitts. These bars had to be "fleeted", that is, shifted, as the barrel slowly turned and the

Fig. 16. Spoke windlass

cable came inboard. In the centre of the main drum, a pawl and ratchet wheel prevented the barrel from "walking back". The barrel was actually designed to turn one way; for heaving only. When the anchor was to be lowered, the depth of the water would be estimated by heaving the lead, and the amount of cable needed to reach the bottom flaked out in front of the windlass. This method, indeed, existed right up to modern times in English coasting schooners and ketches. After the anchor had touched bottom and in order to slack out more cable, an iron bar called a "norman" would be inserted in a hole in the barrel between the part of the cable leading outboard and its next turn around the barrel. This was to prevent "riding turns" being formed as the cable was slacked out. We have evidence that this type of windlass was in use in the thirteenth century, a slightly modified form being found in the days of the galleons, carracks and caravels. The same type is to be seen even today, aboard Chinese junks and Arab dhows.

The next design of this anchor-heaving apparatus was that known as the brake windlass, or as sailors called it the "jiggity-jig wilderness", which appeared about the middle of the nineteenth century. This device lasted on some smaller deep-water ships up to the beginning of the twentieth century, and in coasters up to World War II. It was normally situated under the fo'c'slehead, some ships having

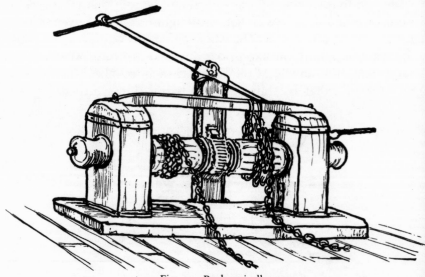

Fig. 17. Brake windlass

a small capstan also on the fo'c'slehead, for use in the operation known as "boarding the fore tack", of which more later. The difference between this windlass and the older pattern was that on either side of the ratchet was fixed a gear wheel with loose pawls, fastened to an athwartship metal rocker-arm or brake (sometimes called a "pump-handle"), with a wooden handle inserted in its outboard end, The pawls would engage the gear wheels when an upward movement was made. Thus the barrel revolved, and hove inboard the anchor cable only when the rocking bars were moved up and down. It was a slow affair, but a great improvement on the old-fashioned handspike windlass of earlier years. In 1851, a fluted barrel which prevented the cable turns slipping came into general use.

The shantyman in earlier times would sit on one of the upright bitts to sing his solos, but in later years, when the crews became smaller, he had to take part in the heaving. However, when he went through the motions of heaving—"riding the bars", it was called— he didn't work too hard, saving most of his wind for the shanty.

The type of shanty sung was a "four-liner"; two lines solos and two lines refrains, a shanty such as *Lowlands* or *Goodbye Fare-ye-well*. Heaving shanties of this kind, a form exactly the same as that of the hauling songs, are definitely the oldest of these shipboard work-songs. And, as in a hauling song, movement would be carried out on certain words. In the case of the windlass songs, however, this movement was done in both the solos and refrains. For instance, the italicised syllables in the following windlass shanty are the ones on which the seamen would jerk the brakes upwards or downwards:

> *Sal*ly *Brown* she's a *fine* mu*lat*ter,
>   *Ch. Way*, *hay*, *roll* an' *go*!
> *She* drinks *rum* an' *chaws* ter*back*er,
>   *Ch. Spends* me *money* on *Sal*ly *Brown*!

Starting with the handle of the brake above their heads (on one side of the windlass, naturally, since the men on the other side would have theirs near the deck) the men would sing "*Sal*" and push the brake down to waist level. On the next heaving word, "*Brown*", they would continue the descent to the deck, coming upwards again on the word "*fine*". The motion of the heaving men was jerky and the rhythm of shanties used for windlass-heaving was jerky also.

The capstan—with an upright barrel, as opposed to the horizontal one of the windlass—was used aboard men-o'-war in the eighteenth century, and in many cases in East Indiamen too. This apparatus, however, was situated neither on nor under the fo'c'slehead but was found, normally, between the fore and main masts. The earliest type

Fig. 18. Wooden capstan

was wooden, with wooden "whelps" (projections) around the barrel in order to prevent the rope cable slipping and causing "riding turns". This type is still occasionally to be found near locks and pierheads of many old docks in Britain and the mainland of Europe. When, in the course of time, larger cables were needed, a nine-stranded cable-laid rope or three right-handed hawser-laid ropes laid up left-handedly were introduced. A cable of these dimensions was found to be too clumsy to go around the barrel of the capstan, so a new system was adopted.

The capstan, a huge affair in the Navy, was placed abaft the main mast, with a smaller capstan some distance from it. The two were united by an endless rope known as a "messenger". The great anchor cable came inboard along the main deck, passing close beside both capstans on its journey to the expansive cable tier beneath the 'tween-decks. In order to heave the cable inboard, it was linked to the messenger by means of short lengths of rope known as "nippers". As the men pushed against the bars of the main capstan (the smaller one was not manned at all) the messenger would begin to move, dragging the nippers along with it, the nippers, in turn, hauling the great cable inboard. As a nipper

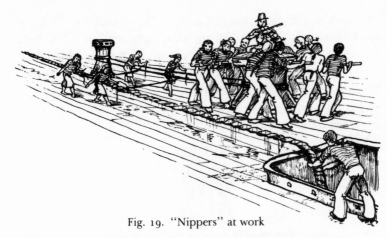

Fig. 19. "Nippers" at work

reached the main capstan it would be fleeted or shifted to its first position near the smaller capstan. This manœuvre was repeated until the job was done. In time, the boy seamen detailed for the job of shifting the nippers were called "nippers" themselves, and it was in this way that the word came to be used for a young boy.

It was on the larger of such capstans that the fiddler or the fifer often sat while playing when the crew hove up anchor.

As chain cable of much smaller circumference than the hemp one became popular, it was taken directly around the capstan barrel when anchor-heaving. However, it was not long before another device took the place of both the great wooden capstan and the wooden barrelled windlass.

Chain cable, which had been out of fashion for centuries, began to return around the beginning of the nineteenth century, and was probably more popular in merchant ships than in men-o'-war. Owing to the fact that much of it was manufactured by piecework families without supervision in Staffordshire backyards, faulty lengths were often linked to the inspected chain of reputable firms and many shipmasters eyed chain with suspicion, preferring the giant hemp cables. With the passing of the Cables and Anchors Act of 1864, which demanded that all links of chain be tested and stamped, the popularity of chain cables grew apace. And with their acceptance came a new kind of windlass. It was made of iron or steel, and in some respects designed in the form of the old-time wooden windlass. In most ships, its position was under the fo'c'sle-head, and in older ships it was flanked by rows of sailor bunks. In place of the old-style horizontal drum, it possessed two large horizontal bobbin shapes (see Fig 20) with "gypsies" or cable-holders in the central part of the bobbins; one to hold the starboard cable, the other to hold the port. Both of these had brake controls and, as in the case of the old barrel windlass, a drum which could be geared for separate working with mooring-lines was attached to a separate axle on the outer side of these cable-lifters. By a series of cogs and

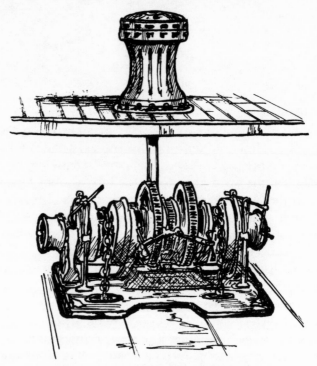

Fig. 20. "Modern" capstan-cum-windlass

worms, the windlass was connected to the main upright shaft of a double-headed capstan up on the fo'c'slehead. When the bars were placed in the lower pigeon-holes only, the capstan itself was used for heaving down the fore-tack (corner of the foresail). But, by dropping a pin from the upper head of the capstan into this lower part and shipping the bars in the upper pigeon-holes, the windlass below would revolve and heave the cable inboard when the men started to heave at the capstan. With this style of windlass-cum-capstan, the chain-locker—instead of being amidships and occupy-

ing a third of the ship's stowage space as did the old hemp cable—
was placed right in the bows of the ship, beneath the men's living
quarters.

Obviously, although a much better system from the point of view
of stowage space, this business of the windlass being inside the
fo'c'sle, with the chain-locker beneath the fo'c'sle deck and the
hawse-pipes, through which the anchor-chain rode, situated right
in the "sharp-end" of the men's living quarters, caused a con-
siderable amount of hardship to the men-before-the-mast. While
the ship was still close to the land, the hawse-pipes had to be left
unplugged in case the anchors were needed. This obviously caused
flooding of the men's accommodation as the ship beat her way
down Channel. Even at sea, after the plugs had been inserted and
caulked with oakum, water still seeped through. In later ships, par-
titions were erected on either side of the windlass, screening off the
port and starboard fo'c'sle from this flooding, the windlass itself
being set in a waterway running out onto the fore-deck.

In some of the later sailing ships, such windlasses were often
made so that they could be steam driven, eliminating "Armstrong's
Patent" entirely. In ships fitted with this kind of windlass, a donkey-
boiler was situated in a house amidships, with a "gypsy" or chain
messenger connecting the windlass with a "niggerhead" or drum
outside the donkey-house bulkhead. However, since a windjammer
could only carry a certain amount of fresh water and not too much
coal, this donkey-boiler was more often than not a white elephant.

The last form of capstan to be evolved was that with the round
head, and this was first used in American ships (Fig. 21). The

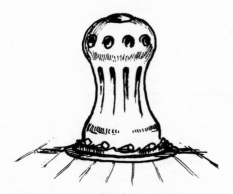

Fig. 21. Roundheaded metal capstan

75

"whelps" already described in the old wooden capstans were, in these newer ones, cast as part of the barrel. The base of any capstan, wood or metal, was fitted with pawls, to provide against "walking back". They could be turned about their pins so as to act in either direction. The pawls geared with the teeth of a rim or pawl-bed secured to the deck. Ships in big swells in ports, such as those of the west coast of South America, have been known to have their capstans strip the pawls and walk back, often maiming or killing the heavers. The older hands, realising that they hadn't so far to walk if they grabbed positions on the bars near to the capstan-head, were usually the ones killed; the younger men, those whose places by tradition were on the outer ends of the bars, were often thrown clear.

It was around this type of capstan that the shanty, as we know it, was sung. The shantyman, unless a ship was well manned, usually "rode the bars" as in windlass-heaving. The shanties sung were of a "rotaty" kind, the jerky ones of the windlass era being unsuitable. But the shantyman, with his native ingenuity, did not take long to adapt these windlass shanties and, by altering the rhythm a little and by adding full choruses, he made many of the old favourites live again.

All this may seem like labouring the point just to show the type of 'machine' at which Sailor John was heaving when he sang his songs! But shanties make more sense when you know how they were used. Then again, an awful lot of nonsense has found its way into print regarding the application of shanties, and I would like to jettison this and put in its place some nautical information nearer to the truth. For instance, there is one forebitter with the following lines:

Scrub the *mud* off of the deadman's face,
An' haul, or ye'll be damned;
For there blows some cold Nor'westers, on
The Banks of Newf'n'land.

I myself have heard singers in folk-song clubs voicing, maybe for dramatic effect, "Scrub the *blood* off of the dead man's face".

I'm sorry to have to kill, in the interests of truth, the dramatic effect of that version of a line from this old forebitter. This "dead man's face" was a triangular piece of metal with three holes in

76

Fig. 22. Deadman's face

it. It was used when mooring ship, when the expectancy of lying in port could be three months or more. Two anchors would be dropped and, to cut the technicalities, their chains would be connected by this piece of metal, and sometimes a swivel, to prevent the two cables becoming twisted round each other during the swinging of the ship on the ebb and flow of the tides. When the chain was hove aboard, it was washed with sea water as it proceeded into the chain locker.

Incidentally, ships do not heave up their anchors, at least, not until the final moment. What happens is this. The ship lies, as in Fig. 23, and when walking round the capstan commences, the ship begins to move towards the anchor, as in Fig 24. The shanties sung while this steady march-round was in progress would normally be faster than those sung as the ship drew nearer her anchor. At first, the shantyman would break forth with something like *South Australia* or *Away for Rio*, turning to *Lowlands* or *Shenandoah* later. When

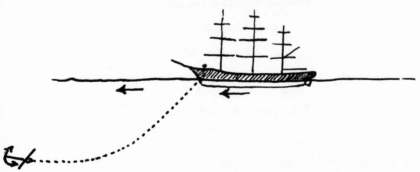

Fig. 23. Heaving-to the anchor

77

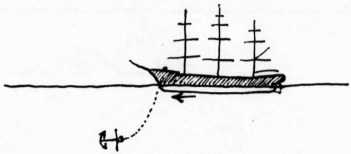

Fig. 24. Heaving-to the anchor

directly over the anchor, singing stopped and then the sing-outs such as "heave 'n she must come!" "Oh, break her out, bullies!" would be voiced. This was necessary in order to get a great concerted effort into breaking-out the "hook" from its slimy and, very often, stubborn resting place. It was, more often than not, a real tussle between the heaving men and the sea-bed, but the men with the aid of their battle-cry, the shanty or sing-out, would eventually win.

The Catting Shanty

The earliest anchor was probably no more than the branch of a tree having an elbow in it with a stone lashed in the elbow to act as a weight. Later, the shape became the more familiar one, but with the

Fig. 25. Early Anchor

"stock" or crosspiece fastened at the base, between the "arms". This type, still found on Chinese junks and cast in metal, is used nowadays for the mooring of buoys. Later still, the great wooden stock anchors came into being—you can see them today aboard Nelson's *Victory*. Many merchant ships carried such anchors. They were known as "Admiralty type" and, with a stock made of metal, continued to be used until the demise of the sailing ship.

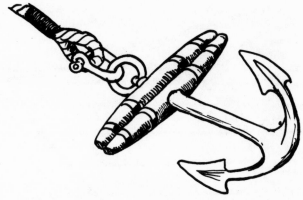

Fig. 26. Wooden stock anchor

Unlike modern stockless anchors used aboard steamers, which can be hove right up into the hawse-pipes, the anchor with a stock had to be "catted and fished". Let me explain this more fully. Most sailing ships had great baulks of oak or teak thrusting out on either bow and bolted to the deck of the fo'c'slehead. These baulks were called "catheads". In olden times, the carved face of a cat was to be found on the outboard end of many of these protuberances.[1] In the older catheads three sheaves were inserted as in a pulley or block. To "cat and fish" the anchor really meant that after the men had hove the anchor "awash", so that it was just touching the surface of the water, an operation was performed in order to bring the anchor up onto the fo'c'slehead so as to stow it. A block with three sheaves and a great hook attached to it would be brought near the cathead and a length of rope rove through this and the sheaves in the cathead. The tackle so formed was overhauled, that is opened out, until the hook could be jerked into the ring of the anchor. Then the men would haul the anchor up—the carpenter slacking out the anchor chain to enable this to be done—until it was hanging "two blocks" under the cathead. This was "catting". The "fishing" consisted of putting the hook under one of the "flukes" or arms of the anchor, and hoisting its lower end up onto the fo'c'slehead, where it would be safely lashed for the rest of the passage.

In later years, a great tackle was used for this operation in preference to rigging the cathead. Its upper end was shackled to the topmast head, and it was called a "fish" or "cat" tackle. To this

[1] They can be seen on the catheads of the *Cutty Sark* at Greenwich.

79

Fig. 27. A cathead, rigged

tackle a long wire pendant with a hook attached was shackled (the "fish-hook") and this was laid in a thumb cleat or "lead" on the cathead in order to guide the hooked anchor up to it. After a few turns of chain were passed through the ring of the anchor to lash it to the cathead, the hook would then be shifted to the opposite end of the anchor in order to fish it. Some ships had an anchor or cat davit standing right up in the bows at the foot of the fore-stay and bowsprit, for the same function. Other ships had a pair of davits on either bow near the catheads. Some more recent ships had a gravity band in the centre of the shank (upright) of the anchor, thus eliminating the double job of cat and fish, bringing the anchor aboard in one movement.

In all the operations of catting and fishing, the fall of the tackle would be taken to the fo'c'slehead capstan, or else manned by hand, and a shanty would be raised as the manœuvre was carried out. A popular catting song was:

> To the cathead, aye yeo,
> *Cheerily man!*
> We'll shift the dead, aye yeo,
> *Cheerily man!*
> She's heavy as lead, aye yeo,
> *Cheerily man!*
> Oh, hauley, aye yeo,
> *Cheerily man!*

As far as I can call to mind, this covers all the anchor operations at which a shanty was sung.

The Capstan Shanty Used for Other Forms of Heaving

The capstan, however, was used for other jobs as well as those connected with the anchor.

The bottom corners of the lowest sails (the courses) were hauled down to the deck by means of ropes called "tacks" and "sheets". When one corner was nearer the wind than the other, the rope or tackle bowsing this to the deck was called the "tack", the rope of the opposite corner being the "sheet". To "board a tack" meant to heave on the tack and bring the "clew" or corner of the lower sail nearer to the deck. When the fore-tack (that of the fore-course) had to be boarded, it was led through a lead-block, usually shackled to the topside of the cathead, and passed several times around the barrel of the fo'c'slehead capstan. This was when the pin that engaged the windlass below the fo'c'slehead would be removed, and the bars inserted in the lower pigeon-holes only. The end of the tack, when the heaving was completed, would be fastened, figure-of-eight fashion, around the fo'c'slehead bitts (the ones from which the word "forebitter" comes). A few stanzas of a capstan shanty would be used for this job.

On the sheet, which would come inboard through the bulwark (rail) of the main deck, the hands would pull directly, and a sheet shanty such as *Haul Away, Joe!* would be sung, with the pull coming on the last word of the refrain. The sheet, in this case, would be a rope of four inches circumference. When wire began to supplant rope to a great extent, it was usual to have sheets and tacks of flexible steel wire. Along with the advent of wire, six main deck capstans were installed, and these were used to bowse down the tacks and sweat in the sheets of all the courses. And so the sheet shanty came to be replaced by a capstan shanty. Incidentally, the fore sheet, being outside the galley door, was known as the "cook's rope". In ships with small crews, these main-deck capstans were often used to take the tops'l halyards to, and here again, instead of a halyard shanty, a capstan song would be raised. Occasionally, the niggerhead messenger would be geared to the capstan and steam used for setting sail, but this method was rare. Even in the sail-carrying passenger steamers of the North Atlantic run, the sails were set by hand and shanties used—men's muscles not costing as much as steam.

As mentioned elsewhere, capstans were sometimes used in the working of the ship's cargo, particularly in timber-carrying ships. In the days before steam winches, the main-deck capstans were much in evidence when warping the ship through the locks and into the docks or when mooring alongside the wharves of the ports of the world.

In some ports, in addition to the mooring lines and wires, the authorities demanded that sailing ships be made fast for'ard by means of the anchor cable. This meant unshackling the chain from the anchor, heaving the chain ashore around a quayside bollard, and back aboard the ship again, where it would be made fast to the bitts. Such an operation was a rather slow continuous job and, as the fo'c'slehead capstan was used, a shanty with many verses or even a lengthy forebitter, such as *The Liverpool Judies*, would be rolled out by the shantyman.

> Singin' ro-o-o-oll, ro-o-o-oll,
> Roll, bullies, roll!
> The Liverpool judies have got us in tow!

A similar operation would take place before reaching port after a long passage. The anchor cable would be hove up on deck, in order to chip and examine it, prior to its being used when the port was reached. For such a manœuvre, the anchor capstan or windlass was used, and a suitable shanty sung. It was in these last two types of capstan work that any old song, so long as it was in march time, would be appropriated by the shantyman.

The Halyard Shanty

Cape Horn, with masts and rigging sheathed in ice; the heaving decks awash. Aloft, the sails belly steadily to the wintry winds. It is eight bells in the middle watch. The fo'c'sle door opens snd spews forth a handful of men, yellow oilskins gleaming from the light of the lantern within. They join their mates near the weather rigging of the mainmast.

"Stand by to set the main upper tops'l!" The stentorian voice of the mate bellows through the Stygian darkness. The yellow-clad figures bend to grasp the huge rope, along which they string like so many outsized wasps.

A lee sea flops aboard, and with a roll envelops the men up to their waists.

"All clear aloft, sir!" comes the shout from high in the darkness. "Right-O! bosun, up with her!" And the men begin to pull on the halyard. Then, from the upright figure, standing dramatically at the forehand of the rope, comes the weird, questioning first line of:

"Say, wuz ye niver darn the Congo River?"

And the yellow oilskinned crew come back with:

"*Blow*, boys, *blow*!"

On the word "blow", they lay back on the rope with a tremendous concerted pull.

"Oh, yes, I've bin darn the Congo River,
Blow, my bully boys, *blow*!"

Inch by inch, foot by foot, the yard is swayed aloft.

That is one of the commonest situations in which a halyard shanty was used.

Unlike capstan songs, which accompanied a continuous exertion, the halyard shanties were used on an intermittent job-o'-work. In order to describe more fully the use of halyard shanties, I should explain, in conjunction with our diagram (Fig. 28), which sails were hoisted and which were not.

Both the lower topsails and the lower top gallant sails (sails with fixed yards) had to be released from their confining ties, known as "gaskets". Their clewlines, which haul up the corners, and the buntlines, which in turn haul up the centre of the sails, would then be thrown off their belayin'-pins and left slack, the sails being then set by hauling on the sheets. The sheets were wire ropes or chains which hauled out the corners of the sails to the ends of the yard beneath. No shanties were needed for this job, nor for the setting of the lower sails or courses, although as already mentioned, a sheet shanty would be used to get the last few pulls on the sheets which were made fast on deck.

The upper topsails and upper top gallant sails, however, were

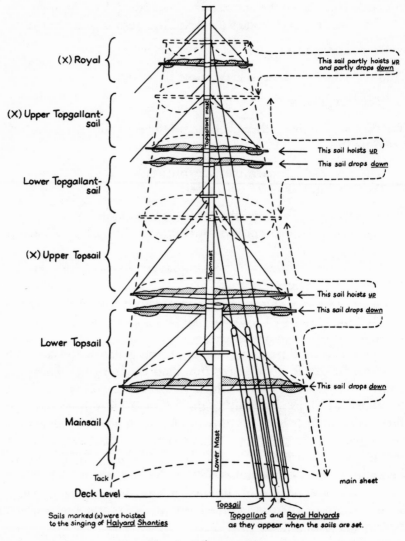

(X) Royal { — This sail partly hoists **up** and partly drops **down**

(X) Upper Topgallant-sail {

Lower Topgallant-sail { — This sail hoists **up** / ← This sail drops **down**

(X) Upper Topsail {

Lower Topsail { ← This sail hoists **up** / ← This sail drops **down**

Mainsail { ← This sail drops **down**

Tack

Deck Level _____ main sheet

Topgallant mast

Topmast

Lower Mast

Topsail

Sails marked (x) were hoisted to the singing of **Halyard Shanties**

Topgallant and **Royal Halyards** as they appear when the sails are set.

Fig. 28. Sail movement

84

sails in which the yards moved up and down the masts, and when setting these a halyard shanty was just the job. The longest task was that of setting an upper tops'l; more rope having to be hauled through the two blocks of its halyard tackle than in the case of the other sails, the blocks having four, or even more, sheaves in each. This chore was, therefore, always accompanied by a long, rambling shanty, such as *Blow the Man Down*. Royals were slightly different to the other sails, being partly lowered and partly hoisted, and usually were so light that they needed nothing more than a sing-out or hand-over-hand shanty at the most.

In old times, single tops'ls, as carried by the early packet ships, and as used in the last men-o'-war of the Sailing Navy, the bottom half of the sail would be dropped and the upper half hoisted. The tops'l halyards would come down from aloft, parallel to the shrouds almost, the lower block being shackled near the waterways or scuppers. The fall, or hoisting part of the tackle, would be led at right angles through a lead-block on deck. The shantyman and perhaps the bosun or second mate would stand at the forehand, that is before the lead block, while the men, with bent backs and bodies low, spread out along the horizontal part of the rope. The shantyman, on being told to "Strike a light!" would, somewhat dramatically perhaps, throw out his arm and, grasping the rope, start at first a running sing-out such as "Oh, lea, ay yu, hay lee, high joo!" in which the men would join. This was known as "dry-pulling". As the sail, the wind filling it, began to belly out from its confined folds, the job would become heavier, and this was when the shanty was needed. Sometimes the shantyman would indicate to the crowd the song he was intending to sing by starting with the refrain first. Two pulls in each refrain was the usual custom, although sometimes, if the shanty was a fast one, a drag on one word of the refrain was sufficient.

The query often asked as to whether a shanty was sung slow or fast has many answers. A lot depended on whether the men were fresh, or whether they had already set many sails, whether the watch below (who had one eye on their bunks) was at the halyards. These and other human frailties have to be taken into consideration in answering this query. But shanties were very rarely sung as slowly as they are often voiced by a "pride" of nautical octogenarians in some "sailor's snug harbour", when labouring forth for the benefit of some enthusiastic shanty collector. It is fairly certain that such men in their prime would have sung much faster and, obviously, in a more virile manner. As to the style of singing; nasal-toned tenor singers, often Americans, Liverpudlians, Irishmen and Cockneys, were preferred as shantymen, although, quite often, Negro, Welsh and Scottish baritones held the field.

The overlapping of the last word or note of the shantyman's solo by the first note of the refrain was a common feature in shantying as in other forms of folk-singing. Wild yelps or breaks in the voice, known to sailors as "hitches", were also often heard. Negro seamen were best at this hitching, with, perhaps, Scandinavian or German seamen a close second. The hitch had no real function other than to give the men a break before coming in again with the refrain. The beginning of the second solo was a common position for the execution of a hitch, as well as on the final note of the first solo. Sometimes it would be used in the middle of the third solo of a hauling or pumping song such as *John Kanaka* or *Mobile Bay*.

> Was yiz never darn in Mobile Bay,
> *John come tell us as we haul away!*
> Screwing cotton of a summer's day,
> *John come tell us as we haul away!*
> Aye, aye, illi-olli aye!
> *John come tell us as we haul away!*

Occasionally hitching would be heard in the refrains. It occurred more frequently in halyard shanties than in capstan songs. Whenever the words "way-hay" or "away" came in a shanty they were usually sung in trilling fashion, and all short "i" sounds such as in "Rio", "early" and "Russian" were sung as "eye", for example "Rye-o", "ear-lye", and "Rushye-an". Words, of course, had to be heard above the soughing of the wind in the rigging, the clacking of the chain sheets, and the rattling of blocks, therefore it was volume and clarity, rather than beauty of tone that were important in shanty singing.

Halyard shanties were also used when bending sail. Before a ship could proceed to sea after she had been lying in port for several months, she had to clothe her naked yards with canvas or "the muslin" as seamen called the sails. When leaving a port in northern Europe or America, a ship would bend her best suit of sails—even a "storm suit"—but when she was nearing the Trade Wind zone, her fine-weather canvas would be bent, that is fastened to the yards. Sails were stowed away down the sail locker, "sausage" fashion. When the day came for bending sail, it was common for a race to take place between the watches, each clothing its own particular

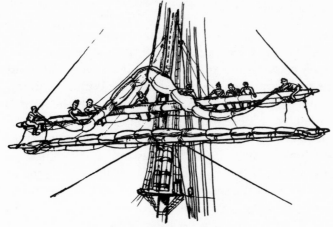

Fig. 29. Bending sail

mast. Gantlines would be sent aloft ready to hoist the sails up to the yards. The sail was hoisted higher than its appropriate yard, its clews (corners) were then hauled out to each yard-arm by the men on the foot-ropes. As it was hauled out and gradually lowered down to the yard, these topmen would fasten the head of the sail to the jackstay (an iron rod on the upper part of the yard) with rope yarns. In the Royal Navy, specially fitted "robands" would be used instead of the merchantman's rather untidy rope yarns.

I remember one morning, having spent the previous night ashore on the ran-tan with some of the lads, opening my bleary eyes and stuffy ears to the raucous voice of our old Cornish bosun chanting:

"Aw, poor ol' Rueben Ranzo,"

and the crowd coming in with the lethal:

"*Ranzo*, boys, *Ranzo*!"

They are bending sail, I thought, and hastily dashed up the fo'c'sle ladder. On reaching the deck, and seeing a row of men in front of me strung out along the gantline as they hoisted the rolled-up sail aloft, I tottered towards them, intent on joining in the shantying. With a yell I disappeared below deck level, landing on a pile of hard canvas down in the chain-locker. Unfortunately for me, the hatch had been left off.

The Pumping Shanty

Of course, pumping, in the days of the wooden sailing ships, was a continuous chore. Even in the composite and later the iron windjammers, a certain time at this miserable task had to be endured.

Of the earliest pumps we know but little. With the coming of the brake windlass, a brake pump, worked in exactly the same fashion as the windlass, was eventually fitted into every ship. Hours would be spent pushing, up and down, the rocker bars or brakes; very often watch and watch, day in and day out.

The pumps were usually situated by the fife-rails of the main or mizen masts. As in the case of the brake windlass, not many hands could get hold of the wooden handles, therefore the men took turn and turn about at the bars. The bosun would shout: "Roll the water-wheel!" and to the query: "Who wuz drunk last?" someone would break forth in song:

> She was just a village maiden wid red an' rosy cheeks,
> *To me, way, hay, hee, high, ho!*
> She went to church an' Sunday school an' sang this anthem
> > sweet,
>
> *There's fy-er darn below!*

The type of shanty sung at the pumps had to be jerky in rhythm to suit the jerky motion of the rocker bars, therefore although there were proper pumps shanties, such as the one given above, those used on the brake windlass were often appropriated for the job, such shanties as *Lowlands*, *Stormalong* and *Goodbye Fare-ye-well*.

> Stormy's gone that good Ol' Man,
> *Timme way you Stormalong!*
> Ol' Stormy's gone that good Ol' Man,
> *Way, ay, ay, Mister Stormalong!*

There was a slight difference in bar movement. In heaving the anchor, the brakes were brought up waist high, and then thrust upwards, level with the shoulders of the men. This constituted two movements. In pumping, the brake was brought from the down to the up position in one movement.

In the second half of the nineteenth century, a new type of pump was installed aboard sailing ships; this was the Downton pump. It had two large flywheels with short handles, allowing no more than two or three men on each. But more men could be used on this type

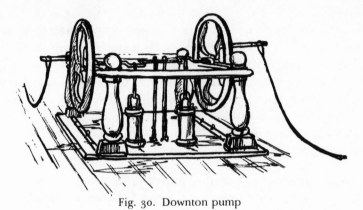

Fig. 30. Downton pump

of pump than on the brake type. A piece of cordage called a bell-rope, with an eye spliced in one end, was dropped over each handle; the one on the starboard side, say, being led for'ard, the one on the port side being led aft. On both these ropes quite a number of men could be employed, one side letting their line slack for a moment, while the others hauled on theirs and drove the flywheels round. What one might call "rotary" songs, as opposed to the jerky brake songs, would be used at the Downton pump. In other words, capstan songs with full choruses, such as *A-rovin'* and *Rio*. But as one old shellback once informed me, "Any old song could be sung at a pump, so long as it had a good rousing chorus!" *John Brown's Body* was a prime favourite:

> John Brown wuz skipper of a Yankee clipper ship,
> John Brown wuz skipper of a Yankee clipper ship,
> John Brown wuz skipper of a Yankee clipper ship,
> As we go rollin' home.
>
> Glory, glory, hallelujah!
> Etc., etc.

Another constant job of work aboard sailing ships was that of "manning the braces". In "tacking" or going about ship, that is, bringing a ship's head through the wind, or its opposite number, "wearing", that is, putting a ship's stern through the wind, the braces were hauled on in order to swing the yards around. To allow all the yards on the masts to swing freely from side to side, the lower sails would be clewed up (their sheets and tacks left slack) with the lee braces also slackened, and the watches would stamp away up the deck hauling on the weather braces. At a certain point in the hauling, as the ship turned, these weather braces would automatically become the lee braces. A description of this stamp 'n' go hauling has been given elsewhere, and it is only necessary to state here the type of shanty used. *Drunken Sailor* was the most popular, although *Hieland Laddie* and *Roll the Old Chariot* were equally well liked by the men.

> And we'll ro-o-oll the ol' chariot along,
> And we'll ro-o-oll the golden chariot along,
> And we'll ro-o-oll the ol' chariot along,
> And we'll all hang on behind!

Around the Equator and in the Doldrums, where squalls of rain, variable light airs and calms are common, this constant hauling on the braces nearly drove the sailorman out of his mind.

There was another job, rarely, if ever, mentioned in shanty books, in which these stamp 'n' go songs were used. That job was scraping the ship's bottom to clean off the barnacles, shellfish and weed-growths. The "devil's instruments" employed were many and varied; each skipper had his own idea as to what was best. These instruments frequently consisted of two or four planks bridled together so that either one or two would lie each side of the keel when eventually hauled into position under the ship. One manœuvre was to haul them sideways from the keel up the ship's sides, but to clean right beneath the ship, the contraption had to be hauled fore and aft. It was when stamping up the deck, usually in a flat calm, dragging this "thing" from for'ard to aft, that a stamp 'n' go song would be raised. Other variations of this instrument resembled giant scrubbing brushes, with stiff bristles covering a wide plank, also with hauling lines coming inboard, and some had metal spikes or wood scrapers protruding from a flat board so as to shift the tough shellfish. Such shellfish and barnacles naturally slowed the progress of a ship, and ships that hadn't got such hell-designed appliances aboard would have the men over the side on stages scraping as far as they could down into the water. This, of course, was before trade unions came along with all sorts of safety measures for seamen.

The Sheet and Bowline Shanty

We have already referred to the sheet or bowline shanty. It was probably the oldest form of true shanty. Several of them still exist, and all of them were used—mainly on the fore and main sheets—when taking a final "jag". This concerted pull always came on the last word, which would be rarely sung or its note given full value, the men gasping forth a wild howl instead.

> Do me Johnny Boker, come rock an' roll me over,
> Do me Johnny Boker, DO!

> Haul on the bowline, Kitty she's me darlin',
> Oh, haul on the bowline, the bowline HAUL!

Perhaps no more than an inch or two would be gained with this final drag, but this would make all the difference to the drawing power of the sail, especially when racing.

The Bunt Shanty

In the packets and the clippers, the system of furling certain sails was different to the method used in the later four-masted barques. Until Admiral Cunningham designed the double tops'l and t'gallants'l, these sails were deeper and therefore had more area of canvas to stow on the yard. The leads of the clewlines and buntlines were also different to those of later ships. This applies to those of the courses or lower sails as well. Sails with these kinds of furling lines were rolled on the yard with what was known as a "bunt stow". A yard was divided into yard-arms and quarters, and the centre was called the "bunt". So this type of stowage meant that the greater bulk of the sail was dragged up on to the yard at its bunt or centre. The clewlines that pulled up the clews of the sail ran across the reverse surface of the sail from clew to bunt, so that when hauled on, the back of the sail would appear as in Fig. 31. The leechlines would drag the "leeches" or sides of the sail in towards the quarters of the yard, and the buntlines would pull the foot of the sail up to the bunt of the yard. After all these lines had been hauled on, the sail

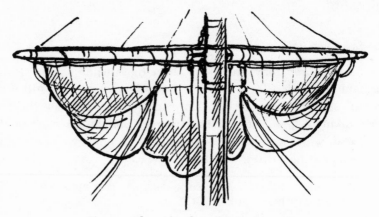

Fig. 31. After side of a sail being bunted

was ready to be "bunted". The men would climb out along the yard, the best sailormen staying in at the bunt, the younger hands posted to the yard-arms where there was not much canvas to stow. This method of stowing a sail was always used in the Royal Navy, where they had a saying, applied to sailormen of little ability, that he was "a yard-arm furler and bunt reefer". In reefing, or shortening the area of a sail when a gale threatened, the best men were stationed at the yard-arms.

The next job in bunting was to get the fold of canvas farthest beneath them into their clutching hands and "skin the rabbit". At this point, in merchant ships, a man would start the shanty *Paddy Doyle's Boots*.

Timme way, hay, hay, hay, aye-yah!
We'll pay Paddy Doyle for his BOOTS!

On the word "BOOTS", all hands would roll the sail up onto the yard. This job, off the Horn, when the sail was wet or frozen, needed herculean efforts on the part of the men to get it stowed, and the invocation of the strange deity Paddy Doyle certainly helped to overcome the power of the Storm Fiend, Boreas. Naturally, in port, this bunt stow would be carried out in a much neater fashion —in what was called a "harbour stow"—than when executed at sea by worn out men in a howling squall of sleet and hail. In the Royal Navy, the job was performed even better, three or four times as many men being on the yard. They would drag the clews or spec-

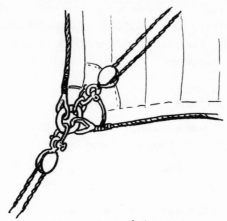

Fig. 32. Spectacle irons

tacle irons (Fig. 32) from under the rear of the yard up to the front and above the yard, forming with the clews what were known as "pig's ears". They would also haul the centre of the bunt up in cone fashion by means of a small tackle or "bunt-jigger" hanging from under the top.

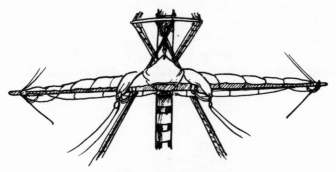

Fig. 33. Pig's ears

93

The earliest form of shantying was that known as the "sing-out". It was primitive and elemental in nature, in all probability imitating the sounds of the wind, sea, creaking hulls and moaning rigging, and it has existed right up to the present day. Even now in this era of atomic ships, one will sometimes hear an older seaman, shipyard or drydock worker give vent to such an eerie cry when hauling on a rope.

Aboard the sailing ships of the nineteenth century, it was to be heard whenever any sort of cordage was hauled upon. When clewing up the lower sails, the hands on deck handling the clewlines, leechlines and buntlines would each howl forth a running hand-over-hand cry:

> Helly holly-high ho, holly hilly, way ya!

Sometimes, as when hoisting stays'ls or jibs, the cry would have some true wording and some musical sense:

> Hand, hand, hand over hand,
> Divil run away wid a Liverpool man!

And even imitated native chants from far-off tropic seas would be roped into use:

> Hairan dairan—arlis—hira bendary—arlis!

As well as these running sing-outs, there were those used for "sweating up". This was a daily routine under sail and meant getting an extra inch on halyard, sheet, tack or brace. One man would keep half a turn of the rope to be sweated under the bottom half of the belayin'-pin, while two or three other hands would stretch their arms as high as they could, grasp the rope, and on a certain word in the chant let fall the full weight of their bodies downwards, finishing by giving every inch of rope gained to the man at the pin. As they dropped they would shout:

> Oh, swig him!
> O-ho, Jew!
> Come 'n' see me!
> Heavy arses!
> Hang me darn!
> O- fiddle-string him!

94

Fig. 34. Swigging

The "Jew" was a memory of an Israelite tailor who may have sold the sailor some shoddy oilskins, and the "Come 'n' see me!" a memory of some seaport Phryne standing on the top step of her brothel with red lips framing an open invitation for Jack to visit her.

At the capstan, too, such self-encouraging semi-chanted cries would be heard:

> Heave and bust 'er!
>
> Roundy, come roundy, for Liverpool town!
>
> Oh, squarey, come squarey!

The Cargo-working Song

In many ports, sailing ships in later days were lucky enough to have their cargoes loaded and discharged by shore gangs and shore cranes, but in earlier days and in ports off the beaten track, the crews with their own ship's gear had to attend to such tasks. We have mentioned the stowing of cotton down hatches, the launching of timber through bowports, and of the chants or shanties sung in each case. In the former, jackscrews, and in the latter, tackles and the capstan were the "mechanical" aids used. Many ships had winches at the foot of the mainmast for use in working cargo; not machinery in the steam or motor sense, but merely contraptions of wooden rollers, cogs and handles. They could be turned in single or double gear and were used for working directly over the hatch. Incidentally, I should mention that hatches of sailing ships were nothing like the great apertures found aboard steamers and motor-ships. They were much smaller and their coamings (sides) were close to the deck.

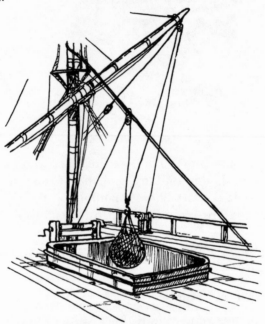

Fig. 35. Yard-arm runner

The main "runner" (Fig. 35) would be worked on such a winch, running aloft from the winch barrel through a "gin-block"—hung halfway down the main stay—and thence down the hatch. A yard-arm runner, shackled to the main runner, would run through an iron gin-block slung from the arm of the cockbilled yard. A cargo-hook would be shackled to the eyes in the working ends of both these runners.

All windjammers would "cockbill" their yards in port for cargo-working, tilting it up in the manner of a crane or derrick. The yard-arm runner, most likely, would be worked from a "dolly-winch" bolted either near the scuppers (waterway) or on the rail itself. Several of these dolly-winches would be used when, for instance, discharging coal on the coast of Chile. They were portable and consisted of a single barrel, no gears and drums outside the uprights.

The yard-arm runner worked the cargo to and from the quayside; the main runner (on the winch) worked the cargo into and out of the hold. Even nowadays, the phrase "yard-arm runner" is used on all docksides for the derrick swinging out over the wharf.

At this type of winch (not the dolly-winch), songs would be raised, and as the work was of a rotary kind, shanties of the capstan type, pumping ditties and shoreside songs with good choruses would be sung in a day's work by the heavers.

Chants, now lost, were also sung by seamen when swinging the heavy "commanders" or wooden mallets with which they hammered into position the bags of saltpetre down the stuffy holds of their vessels on the Flaming Coast of Chile. Miss C. Fox Smith has saved the only surviving one, which runs:

> There goes *one*,
> Hurrah, my boys, strike *one*,
> For one now is *gone*,
> And there's many more to *come*,
> For to make up the *sum*,
> For one hundred so *long*. (*Ad lib.*)

The men would strike the bags with their commanders on the italicised word at the end of each line. Those readers who have seen the performers striking their hammers and singing the *Anvil Chorus* in the opera *Il Travatore* will be able to get a clear picture of this chore as performed by sailormen years ago.

Songs at the Brace and Halyard Winches

In the last of the four-masted barques to be built, Jarvis brace and halyard winches were a great innovation. Brace winches, being situated in positions near the masts, greatly reduced the need for men to have to wade waist-deep in icy water when performing the operation known as "lee fore brace", although a final pull was usually needed on the rope "stretchers" on the rail. The halyard winches, on the other hand, sometimes jammed when a ship was rolling heavily, and the writer, having been shipmates with both rope-tackle halyards and halyard winches, has often felt that the men preferred the tackles to the winches. Only four or five men could get on the handles of this kind of winch, the turning of which was far heavier work than a straight pull on a four-fold purchase. Sometimes a song would be sung at such winches, but more often than not, the men were far too short of wind to do any singing.

Ceremonial Shanties

A shanty devised entirely for ceremonial purposes was that called *The Dead Horse* or *Poor Old Man*.

Merchant seamen in the sailing-ship days were given an "advance note" (an advance of their wages, usually of one month, but sometimes as much as three) ostensibly to enable them to purchase oilskins, seaboots, "donkey's breakfasts", woolly underwear and so on, for a Cape Horn passage. However, sailors of those days, being what they were, very rarely put the "note" to such good use. Instead, they handed it to the crimps or boarding-house masters and had a percentage of its value in booze and women. This, of course, is often referred to in the old forebitters. Often, for the first month, the sailor considered he was working for nothing; "working for a dead horse" as the saying goes. At eight bells, in the second dog-watch, on the last day of being a month at sea, the hands would muster on deck to enact the Ceremony of Paying-off the Dead Horse.

A few days previously, the sailmaker would have cut out from old canvas an effigy of a horse, and this he stuffed with "rounding" (old rope) and a couple of holystones (sandstone used for scrubbing the decks).

First, the "horse" would be hauled along the deck to the break of the poop, where the Old Man, if he was a sea-dog of the old tradition, would give each man a tot of rum. Then, the horse would be attached to a gantline, the gantline being rove through a block on the main yard-arm. Up aloft, the youngest member of the crew would be sitting athwart the yard with a knife in his hand. On the word of command, the men would grasp the gantline, running

98

through a lead-block on the deck, and the shantyman would start the shanty dedicated to this job:

Oh, I say ol' man yer horse will die,

and the crowd would yell:

An' we *say* so, an' we *hope* so!

pulling aloft the horse on the words "say" and "hope". There were many verses to this song, in order to make it last until the horse reached the yard-arm. Then, with much cheering, the lad aloft would cut the gantline and the horse would drop into the "drink". After this ceremony, the men would work with a will, believing that, for the first time, they were really being paid for their work. Incidentally, this ceremony lasted right to the end of Sail, whereas the famous Crossing the Line ritual died out entirely in merchant ships, being revived only in modern passenger liners.

Another Ceremony, that of opening the first barrel of "junk" or "salt horse" for the voyage, was also accompanied, not by a shanty, but by a chant. Salt meat was stowed in harness casks, the "horse in its harness", but before it reached the harness cask, it was put aboard in barrels. Every so often, one of these barrels would be opened and the stringy-looking flesh put into the harness cask with added salt water. On the opening of the first of these barrels, the sailors would gather round with long faces and, in the manner of a Gregorian chant, voice the following:

> Salt horse, salt horse, we'd have ye know,
> That to the galley ye must go;
> The cook without a sign of grief,
> Will boil ye down an' call ye beef,
> An' we poor sailors standing near,
> Must eat you though ye look so queer.
> Salt Horse, salt horse, what brought ye here?

And, finally, there was what may be called the Paying-off Shanty, *Leave Her, Johnny, Leave Her*. This was sung in one form at the final pumping out of a wooden ship or, in another form, at the making fast of the ship alongside in her final port.

Next day would be pay-day at the shipping office with, in

sequence, booze and girls, and so the future looked rosy. Maybe the crimps and runners and other predatory shore types would have tumbled over the rail "to give the boys a hand" and to hand out the rotgut liquor. Anyhow, it was the happiest day of the voyage, and must be celebrated accordingly. Although there was an unwritten rule among merchant seamen that a sailor could sing in his shanty all about his hates and vicissitudes, his dislike of the after-guard, the lousiness of the grub, the meanness of the owners and his abhorrence of the "bloodboat" he had been unfortunate enough to sign in, he rarely took advantage of this licence during the voyage. There were many sea-miles yet to go, and the Old Man could get nasty. Such declarations were saved for the final shanty. In *Leave Her, Johnny, Leave Her* the sailor released his pent-up feelings and really "went to town", knowing full well he would be clearing the ship and its hazing afterguard within a few hours. One of the more printable verses runs:

> Oh, pray may we, never be,
> *Leave Her, Johnny, leave her!*
> In a hungry bitch the likes o' she,
> *An' it's time for us to leave her!*

Fig. 36. Leave her, Johnny

Coasting Songs

I have often been asked whether shanties were sung aboard coasting sail in the old days. The answer to this is that they may have been, depending on the date and type of coaster.

A paragraph in the book SHIPPING WONDERS OF THE WORLD reads:

"The sailing coasters were often slipshod in their shanties because they didn't carry enough men. Although they had a number of shanties, these were seldom heard in deepsea ships, and the usual habit was to adopt the music-hall ditties of the day."

There may be some truth in this, but certainly not with regard to the coasting schooners and ketches of the British coast. In earlier ships however, such as the Geordie coal brigs and the pit-prop or

Fig. 37. Geordie brig

"Baltic" carriers, shanties may have been sung and possibly music-hall ditties were adopted. *The Drummer and the Cook*, first given in print by Terry,[2] is probably one of the latter. The north-east coast version of *Billy Boy*, too, is probably a shanty hailing originally from coasters and before that from shoreside.

Of course, coasting men and fishermen had their own songs of leisure, such songs as *Windy Weather*, *The Fishes* and *Still I Love Him*, possibly of net-hauling origin. My friend Bob Roberts, of the sailing barge *Cambria*, has quite a collection of these East Anglian coast and fishermen songs. And through traditional singers, such as Sam Larner and Harry Cox, many more have been saved. As well as

[2] THE SHANTY BOOK, Part 1.

101

those songs that the coasting sailorman, bargeman and fisherman can claim as their own, there are several deepwater songs that have been taken and trimmed to suit the trades which such men served. By comparing a line from the deepwater version and a similar line

Fig. 38. Sailing barge

from the coast version of the old forebitter *Maggie May*, the "folk process", as the subtle altering of folksongs is known, can be plainly seen.

Deepwater:

I paid off at the Home, after a voyage from Sierra Leone.

Coast:

I paid off at Rotherhithe, from a trip way north of Blyth.

In the New World, it would also appear that shanties were occasionally sung in coasting sailing ships, but the material collected is rather sparse at present, and is open to some future collector with his nose to the ground, or as sailors say, "his ventilators on the wind". However, in THE MINSTRELSY OF MAINE, one coastwise shanty has been saved. It was obtained from Capt Rufus H. Young of Maine, who said it was a "favourite shanty for getting under way" and had upward of forty or fifty verses. It went to the tune of *When Johnny Comes Marching Home* and was called *Johnny, Fill Up the Bowl*:

> Johnny and Jenny by the fireside sat,
> > Hoorah! Hoorah!
> Johnny and Jenny by the fireside sat,
> > Hoorah!...

Forebitters

We have referred to forebitters many times in these pages, but as yet we have not examined the traditional ways in which Sailor John sang them.

Some older readers will remember the almost traditional manner in which the "pub-closer" *Nelly Dean* was sung:

> There's an ol' mill by the stream, Nellie Dean-ah.

To omit the final drawn out "ah" was almost a sin. And so, too, in the singing of forebitters this final "ah" was rarely omitted. Ashore, years ago, rural singers, such as the peasant in his fields, the villager in his tavern, the parish clerk leading hymn-singing, and the wandering minstrel, all had a certain style of high-pitched nasal singing in which before words containing a double "l" a "d" would be placed. The sailor, when singing his forebitters, also employed this interpolated "d"; he sang "rodling" for "rolling", "travedling" for "travelling", "pidlow" for "pillow", and so on. Long after this style of singing had died out ashore, Sailor John continued to insert extra sounds in such words as "haul" ("audle"), "believe" ("budlieve"), "awhile" ("a-whiddle"), "afraid" ("afferaid"), and so on. And in forebitters, as well as in shanty singing, the short "i" was always sung as "eye". The interpolating of a letter, or even a syllable, needed an extra note or two, usually grace-notes (extra notes sung before some notes which are necessary to the tune), to carry the insertion. Grace-notes and rapid quavers were heard far more in the forebitters than in the shanties, and although the reason was mainly on account of these insertions, another explanation is possible. As stated elsewhere, many forebitters came from Irish sources. In Ireland and Scotland, when a fiddler was absent and a jig desired, or when the fiddler had had an overdose of potheen, "mouth-music" was the order of the day. This mimicry of the fiddle's sound may have been taken to sea along with the Irish airs often used by seamen. Consequently, the innumerable grace-notes and rapid ornamenting notes, and the falsetto style of singing with which Sailor John embellished his forebitters, may have been little more than his rendering of the actual sound of the fiddle strings or the wailing of the pipes.

A landlubber hearing an old shellback singing a forebitter with many twiddles and embellishments may believe that these are signs of senile decay, but in fact, all sailing-ship men, whether young or old, first tripper or seasoned voyager, have always sung in this traditional manner.

A type of nautical song to which we have as yet given no space is the humorous or nonsense song. And, believe me, sailors did have fo'c'sle songs which can be described as humorous. One of the first to come to mind is a parody on the old transportation ballad, *Ten Thousand Miles Away*:

A twin-screw brig, with an A.1. rig, was the good ship *Bolivar*,
All spick an' span, from the donkey-man, to the bilge in the
capstan bar;
She was bully-hauled with a ten-foot yawl and a regular hobo
crew,
And right abaft on the mizenmast the scarlet bosun flew.

Ch. Sing blow ye winds high ho!
A-rovin' we will go,
We'll stay no more on England's shore, to hear sweet
music play,
We're off on the mornin' train, to cross the ragin' main,
We're off to my love, with a boxin'-glove, ten thousand
miles away.

We took a reef in the mizen-top, ran out the spanker boom,
Then smartly hauled the keel on deck, to give the mainmast
room;
The tiller was lashed to the starboard bow, and the bowsprit
trailed behind,
Whilst all the crew, so brave 'n' true, were three sheets in the
wind.

Another popular one was:

On the fourteenth of December, boys, it was our sailing day,
And we sailed away from Frisco town, an' we all felt blithe an'
gay,
For our cargo it was colza-oil, bound round for Sandy Hook,
An' there wasn't a man on board the ship knew where to find
the cook.

A similar nonsense song was sent me by Capt S. C. Smith of Hong
Kong, one-time apprentice in the barque *Inverclyde*:

It was on the fifteenth of November, so well I do remember,
So well I do remember,
It nearly broke my poor old mother's heart;
For I signed on with the skipper of a big four-masted clipper,
To sail round the north and foreign parts—Woollamaloosh!

Ch. Oh, the windy winds did blow, and the rain and blindin'
snow,
And a devil of a hurricane did blow-o-oh!
And it nearly knocked the stuffin' out of the good ship
Ragamuffin,
As off to the tropics we did go—Woollamaloosh!

Unfortunately, Capt. Smith had forgotten the rest of this interesting
bit of nonsense. Another funny and, in the original, slightly bawdy
ditty, probably heard more in the half-deck among the apprentices
than from the men in the fo'c'sle, is:

There was a four-wheeled craft,
An' her rig was fore 'n' aft,
When a fire went a-sailin' by;
An' the wind blew off the skipper's wooden leg,
Then we hung the skipper out to dry.
He looked so very sick, we had to rub him with a brick,
An' wash his sweaty feet with ham 'n' egg.

Ch. Singin', lower down the funnel, stop the ship,
An' reef yer anchor-chain;
Throw the maindeck overboard,
An' haul it back again;
Trice yer wash-ports up aloft,
While the stormy winds do blow;
For the ship struck a rock,
An' it burnt a sailor's cock,
Yo-Ho, me lads, yo-ho!

Fig. 39. Apprentices in the half-deck

Odds and Ends

In the past, many other classes of tradesmen connected with the sea in various ways have sung songs and shanties while at work, but this is a field as yet untrodden by the collector and it is doubtful whether such songs will ever be recovered now; it is too late. I am thinking, for example, of the boatmen of the world, and the songs they sang when rowing in order to keep the stroke. There are a few songs collected in France, Sicily and the Hebrides, but there is very little else. Dana mentions boat songs in his TWO YEARS BEFORE THE MAST, but unfortunately he failed to record their words, music or even their titles in his journal.

Then there are the work-songs which we know were sung by the men and women who toiled at rope-making in the roperies of the ports, but none has been handed down to posterity. These crafts-men, men and women, would walk back and forth, covering miles in the course of a working week, twisting the cordage into shape—running rigging for merchantmen, great cable-laid hawsers for the Navy, as thick as a man's body, and whalelines for the Greenland Fleet. And as they walked and worked they sang. Memories of the long roperies along which they plodded are kept alive in such street names as Cable Street and Rope Walk in Wapping and Limehouse, London; in Cable Street, Liverpool; in The Canne-bière in Marseilles, and the Reeperbahn in Hamburg.

Shipyard workers, too, apparently sang shanties or work-songs of some kind. I have before me Vol. 13 (January, 1952) of the ex-cellent little nautical magazine, SEA BREEZES. In an article on old shipyards, the writer Mr A. D. Browning, calls to mind a coastal shipyard at Clymping, near Littlehampton, and the big flywheel the shipyard gang had to turn in order to warp schooners and ketches on a cradle up the slipway. He comments: "This was a laborious and lengthy procedure, and was accompanied by a chanty with the words:

> Round goes the wheel, troubles I defy;
> Jogging along together, my boys,
> The old grey mare and I."

That was in the 1890s, and I was rather thrilled to find that the shipyard of which he writes was the one which built the wooden sailing ship *Leading Light*, an ancient craft in which I once made a pleasant passage out to Demarara, British Guiana.

Fig. 40. Naval ship of the transitional era

A year or so ago I corresponded with Mr F. A. Cluett, an ex-naval seaman of the "down funnel, up screw, make sail!" era, a time when naval ships were in the transitional stage, being fully rigged with squaresail, either as ships, barques or barquentines, each having steam power as well. As the hulls of such ships were of iron they needed constant chipping, and in connection with this Mr Cluett mentioned a type of song I had never even heard of—"paint-chippers". He said that there were dozens of these songs which were sung by the men on stages over the ship's side to help to keep the strokes of the chipping-hammers in unison. As most of

them were bawdy, however, they have never seen the light of print.
I give one of the least offensive here in order to show the type of
song used:

Why sailors, why sailors, got no money to spend?
The White Man took my silver, and the Black Man took my
brass,
The White Man kissed my ruby lips, and the Black Man
kissed . . .
Why sailors (*repeat*) . . .

Pilot Verses

Around our coasts and those of Newfoundland and Canada too,
the often half-literate or even totally illiterate seamen and skippers
of coasting craft invented "songlets" or rhymes, which were often
referred to as "pilot verses". Many a good ship was saved from
finding a hard bottom because the captains and the mates com-
mitted to memory these brief verses. Unfortunately, very few of
these ditties have survived. Here are two, once used on the eastern
coasts of England; the first for ships northbound:

First the Dudgeon, then the Sperm,
Flamboro' Light comes next in turn;
Scarboro' Light stands out to sea,
And Whitby Light bears northerly.
Huntly Foot that damned high land,
Is five and twenty from Sunderland.

the second for south-bound ships:

Roker, Whitby, Flamboro', Spurn,
Outer Dowser, next in turn,
East Dudgeon and Cromer bold,
Look out for Haisboro' and the Wold;
Then Kentish Knock, the Goodwins three,
North, East and South, in turn you'll see.
Then Dover with its cliffs so white,
Dungeness and Sovereign now in sight,
Beachy and Owers, stream the log,
Down the Channel, clear of fog.
Point to point, and light to light,
We'll sail along both day and night.

A Newfoundland set of pilot verses, called *Wadham's Song* and sung to the tune of *I'll Tell Ma, When I Get Home* was put on record in the Admiralty Court, London, soon after it was composed (1756), being considered the best coasting guide up to that time for that wild and rugged shore. Here are the first two verses:

From Bonavista to the Cabot Isles, the course is north full
forty miles,
When you must steer away nor'-east, till Cape Freals, Gull Isle,
bears west-nor'-west.
Then nor'-nor'-west thirty-three miles, three leagues off shore
lies Wadham's Isles,
Where of a rock you must beware, two miles sou'-sou'-east
from off Isle bears.

Newfoundland makes one think of seals. Now although many whaling songs have been preserved and are still sung in the folk-clubs today, songs from the crews of sealers are noticeably absent. To the best of my knowledge no book has ever appeared purporting to be SONGS THE SEALERS SANG and I know of no sealing song to be included in the numerous books on sea-songs, forebitters, shanties and so on, nor in the ordinary folk collections. However, when I was gathering material for my own book SHANTIES OF THE SEVEN SEAS, a certain Mr D. MacDonald of Glasgow lent me a most interesting and extremely rare pamphlet of songs sung by the old-time sealers,[3] published in St John's, Newfoundland, in 1925. Although only text is given, the tune of each song is named, usually some well-known air. Here is a sealing song from this collection, a typical come-all-ye of the early 1840s:

Tom Casey being commander of the *St Patrick* called by name,
With twenty-eight as brave a boys, as ever ploughed the main,
It was upon the 1st of March, from Carbonear we set sail,
Wind from the west-sou'west, my boys, a smart and pleasant
gale.

And here is another with very technical words:

With knife and fork, with kettle and pan,
With spoon and mug and glasses,
To shield our eyes from glaring sun,
And to take our tea with 'lassies'.

[3] SONGS SUNG BY THE OLD-TIME SEALERS OF MANY YEARS AGO, compiled and published by James Murphy (St John's, Newfoundland, Feb. 1925).

Ch. For we are 'swoilers', toilers bold,
   And we copy from pan to pan, sir,
   With pelts astern we shipward go,
   Nor yield to any man, sir.

Fig. 41. Sealing schooner

These songs, unlike many of the whaler songs already referred to, were not the work of shore ballad-makers but, from their terminology and style, obviously real forebitters put together by the sealers themselves.

There is one form of nautical work-song which apparently has never existed among English-speaking sailormen and longshore workers. This is the ballast-throwing song, once known down the holds of ships from the mainland of Europe and on the wharves of Rotterdam and Oslo. Miss Laura Smith has one or two of these in her international collection of sailor songs[4] as well as having a "splicing song" in French—although, as an erstwhile seaman, I have not the slightest clue as to why a man splicing a rope had any need for a song to help him tuck over and under. Miss Smith also has "holystoning songs" from Russia and Japan in her fine collection, but as yet, I have been unable to discover whether such songs were ever used by English-speaking sailormen.

[4] MUSIC OF THE WATERS.

SHANTY COLLECTORS, BOOKS AND RECORDS

The earliest collectors of shanties—those, that is, who put them into books—were Miss Laura Alexandrine Smith and Capt. Frederick Davis. Cecil J. Sharp too, probably the greatest of all folk-song collectors, was intensely interested in the sailor shanty and was one of the early collectors. Many of his collected items have never seen print, his original manuscript collection being on the shelves of the Clare College Library, Cambridge University. In the JOURNAL OF THE FOLK-SONG SOCIETY are to be found some shanties from his collection, and in 1914 he published his book ENGLISH FOLK-CHANTEYS, containing the more popular items.

Sharp obtained many of his shanties from an old sailor called John Short of Watchet, Somerset, from whose singing Sir Richard Runciman Terry also transcribed many shanties for his work THE SHANTY BOOK. This book was published in two parts, the first in 1921 and the second in 1926. In November 1917 he wrote the article "Sailor Shanties" in THE MUSIC STUDENT and, in 1919, his A FORGOTTON PSALTER was published by the Oxford University Press.

John Short had a good repertoire. He had sailed in British and American sailing ships. He served in the Yankee ship *Levant*, in 1866, at the time of the American Civil War, and during that time he got his nickname of "Yankee Jack" which stuck to him all his life. A comparison of the shanties obtained from him by both famous collectors will at once show the difficulty of getting a one-tune, one-set-of-words shanty on different days and under different circumstances, from the same seamen. The songs of Short differ in the works of both Sharp and Terry, sometimes considerably. The writer is aware that he, too, has this loose, variable way of delivering his shanties to audiences, and he doubts if he ever sings them quite the same way twice. But then this is folk-singing as opposed to "art-singing". As well as various seamen singing the same shanty in many different ways, shanties in various coastal areas also varied greatly in both words and music. Those from the Tyne would differ from those of Liverpool, where shanties in turn would vary slightly from those of London and widely from those of the Bristol Channel ports. And American seamen had their own versions.

Terry, perhaps unfortunately, tackled this problem forcibly, like a true man of music maybe, but certainly not as a folk-song collector. Apropos a certain shanty he declared that "there must necessarily be some means of getting at the tune, unhampered by these individual idiosyncrasies . . .", and with this in mind, he worked patiently at sorting out from various deviations what, in his view, was the real tune of each shanty which he then transcribed on paper for ever.

Sharp, on the other hand, was not hampered by this phobia. He transcribed every shanty variant he ever came across, therefore being more true to the shanty, and giving posterity a collection far more valuable to the student and folk-singer than that of Terry.

However, by a twist of fate, it was Terry's collection that was accepted by schools and by baritone singers of the 1920s, the result being that his version of a certain shanty is the one generally found in circulation today. But in the folk-song clubs of the present time, Sharp's versions are at last beginning to come into their own.

The collection of Capt. F. Davis has often been decried by other collectors as somewhat spurious. In particular, Davis has been accused of altering the texts of his shanties, not just camouflaging bawdy phrases and so on, but rewriting whole shanties. This accusation is entirely unjustified to my way of thinking. The cap may fit two or three of his shanties, but no more. In fact I have always thought his collection to be one of the best, and I am fairly certain that a certain Comdr. Woollard, an old sea-dog still on deck and well-known to the Cape Horn Society, would agree with me entirely. I believe he always used Davis's book when lecturing on this subject.

Miss L. A. Smith was a contemporary of Davis, although the area in which she collected British shanties was that in which Terry also obtained many of his—the north-east coat area. However, her book, until publication of my SHANTIES FROM THE SEVEN SEAS, was the only one which made any attempt at being international. In spite of many *faux pas*, her great collection, THE MUSIC OF THE WATERS, is a most valuable work and much that is rare can be gleaned from her pages. This book came to be written through an idea of Major E. R. Jones, who was the United States Consul in Cardiff and also editor of THE SHIPPING WORLD in the last quarter of the nineteenth century. His idea of a collection of sailor songs of all nations arose from his almost daily contact with ships and sailors of many countries. The result was that he commissioned Miss Smith on behalf of his paper to write a series of articles containing specimens of the shanties of each maritime country. These articles were later expanded and became the fine volume THE MUSIC OF THE WATERS. In those days, unfortunately, the art of folk-song collecting was in its infancy and much rubbish was included with the good material. This is true of Miss Smith's work. *The Eton Boating Song* would probably be jettisoned by a modern publisher from a work purporting to be a sailor-song book nowadays. But if it hadn't been for such early collectors as Miss Smith, many shanties (especially those plagiarised by later collectors) would never have survived to the present day. To Miss L. A. Smith, Capt. Davis and Cecil Sharp we owe a great debt. Two other collectors of the 1880s, who did not publish books on the subject, are W. L. Alden and James Runciman. Alden wrote an article called "Sailor Songs" in HARPER'S NEW MONTHLY MAGAZINE in 1882. Also, his article "Sailors' Shanties and Sea-Songs" appeared anonymously in CHAMBERS'S JOURNAL as early as 1869. James Runciman published in ST JAMES' GAZETTE a fine article on sailor songs with musical items. In 1904, J. Bradford and A. Fagge between them published a good, though comparatively small, collection of shanties, very authentic and sailor-like.

L. G. Carr Laughton was probably the first writer to unroll the historical backcloth of the shanty. And he was the first to point out the effects of the cotton trade from the Southern States on the development of the sailor work-song.[1]

An important name in connection with early research into shantying around the ports of the Mediterranean is that of Miss Lucy E. Broadwood. She gave her findings on pages 55–58 of Vol. 8 of the JOURNAL OF THE FOLK SONG SONG SOCIETY. The article is divided into two parts: (1) "On the Aegean Sea (200–400 A.D.)" and (2) "On the Adriatic (1480–1483 A.D.)".

[1] "Shantying and Shanties", MARINERS' MIRROR (Vol. 9, 1923).

It will be noted that, apart from Capt. Davis, seamen are not in evidence during the early days of shanty research, collecting and publishing. Around the second decade of the present century several now well-known sailor names came to the fore. Capt. W. B. Whall brought out his SHIPS, SEA SONGS AND SHANTIES in 1910, a volume containing all the material from articles he had written in THE NAUTICAL MAGAZINE during the years 1906, 1909 and 1910. He had an excellent background for his work in this field. He spent eleven years in the old passenger-carrying East Indiamen, during which time he took down the words and music of these songs as they were actually sung by sailormen in the China and Australia trades. During his early years at Oxford University, he received a thorough musical training under Sir John Stainer, who was later the organist of St Paul's Cathedral. Whall doesn't tell us whether he was ever a shantyman himself, but our next collector most certainly was. This one-time seaman and ex-whaler is Frank T. Bullen and his book SONGS OF SEA LABOUR (1913) was the first to note in detail the connection between Negro work-songs and the white sailors' shanties. He spent much time around the West Indies and the Guianas where he picked up many unusual shanties. Having been a shantyman, he realised the impossibility of putting in print the whole of any shanty as sailor-sung, contenting himself by giving the first verse and tune of each shanty only.

John Masefield, another ex-seaman and the late Poet Laureate, wrote an article called "Sea Songs" published in the magazine TEMPLE BAR in 1906, and in 1924 he brought out his book A SAILOR'S GARLAND. This latter contains many sea-songs and shanties, unfortunately without their tunes.

In America, the earliest collector in print was another ex-seaman, Capt. John Robinson. In the now defunct magazine THE BELLMAN, he wrote several articles on shantying, giving many musical examples, including two or three shanties not found in other collections. He was born an Englishman, but our next collector is American. This is Miss Joanna C. Colcord who, I believe, is still with us, but bears a married name now. She was born at sea aboard her father's ship which was engaged in the China trade. She is a descendant of a long line of New England deep-water sailormen. The majority of the shanties in her book ROLL AND GO she heard herself on shipboard, and therefore they have the brand of authenticity about them. This book was published in Indianapolis in 1925, an enlarged edition being published in 1938, in New York. This latter is called SONGS OF AMERICAN SAILORMEN, and it includes forebitters ("mainhatch songs" as the Americans called them), whalers' songs and the songs of the fresh-water sailors of the Great Lakes. This last group of songs has no counterpart in any other printed collection.

In 1913, J. E. Patterson, another ex-seaman, brought out his THE SEA'S ANTHOLOGY (New York), a volume containing many shanties without tunes, and in the 1920s Frank Shay, another seaman, published a collection of shanties called IRON MEN AND WOODEN SHIPS (New York and London). These were the worthwhile American collections until William Main Doerflinger brought out his great work SHANTYMEN AND SHANTY-BOYS (New York) in 1951. He was probably one of the first folk-song collectors deeply interested in the sailor work-song to use the tape recorder. He recorded the fine shanty-man Dick Maitland, Capt. Henry E. Burke and Capt. Patrick Tayluer, excellent repositories of the shanty and forebitter. From the singing of other seamen too, men like John O'Brien, William Laurie and Harry Steele of "Sailors' Snug Harbour", Doerflinger recorded many fine salt-water items which he has included in his book. Two interesting chapters in Doerflinger's work are "Ballads of the Fishing Banks", dealing with the songs sung by the cod and halibut fishermen of the Grand Banks, and "Forecastle Songs of the West Indies Trade", forebitters sung aboard the brigs, barquentines and schooners engaged in trading between Canada and Nova Scotia and the Caribbean. One more American seaman, now deceased, to whom we must most certainly refer is Frederick Pease Harlow, who spent many years in the sugar trade out in the East Indies. His collection of shanties and sea-songs was first published in the magazine AMERICAN NEPTUNE (Salem, Mass.) in April 1948. In 1962, this was enlarged and published as a book under the title CHANTYING ABOARD AMERICAN SHIPS (the Barre Publishing Company Incorporated, Barre, Mass.). Many unusual shanties are given as well as whaling songs and forebitters. The only quarrel I have to pick with Harlow lies in his frequent statement that pulls were given in the solo as well as in the refrain lines of hauling songs, and he marks his songs accordingly with *sforzando* marks (>). This may have occurred in his ship, but he is entirely wrong if he believes that this practice was carried out in all other ships.

In the 1920s and 1930s many shanty books appeared in Britain. In 1927, Miss C. Fox Smith brought out her A BOOK OF SHANTIES. She was a highly gifted nautical writer and sea-song lover, whom PUNCH declared must have possessed the combined souls of many old shellbacks to be able to write about sailing ships in the way she did. In the same year, John Sampson, an ex-seaman, published his THE SEVEN SEAS SHANTY BOOK, the shanties from which were used by the members of the Seven Seas Club, London, in an attempt to bring down the rafters of their meeting place. In 1931, Capt. David W. Bone brought out his discursive CAPSTAN BARS, giving a fine background to the shanties, but containing very few musical items. In 1928, Rex Clements, another old sailorman, published his MANAVILINS, a fine volume containing many forebitters. Seamen, and particularly apprentices, used the word "manavilins" for the leftovers from the cabin table, which the cabin steward, if in a generous mood, would slip surreptitiously to them when the afterguard had finished eating.

Regarding books containing sea-songs and forebitters, but not entirely devoted to these, the earliest British one to be recommended to the student of sea-song is John Ashton's REAL SAILOR SONGS of 1891 (I don't agree, however, that all the songs included are "real" sailor-songs). This was the first genuine attempt to bring together sailor come-all-yous, forebitters and ballads, in one book.

For naval songs and ballads, EARLY NAVAL BALLADS OF ENGLAND by J. O. Halliwell, published for the Percy Society in 1851, and C. H. Firth's NAVAL SONGS AND BALLADS, printed for the Navy Records Society in 1908, are both mines of information. Christopher Stone's SEA SONGS AND BALLADS (Oxford, 1906) is another fine collection. Unfortunately, these four collections do not give any tunes to the songs. Those from broadsheets do have the name of the tune to which the ballad should be sung, but these are, in most cases, of even earlier vintage than the words of the ballad. The ballad may be of the seventeenth or eighteenth century, but its appropriate tune may be from the fifteenth or sixteenth century and such tunes are generally difficult to trace or even lost for ever. Three other good British books are Mrs Clifford Beckett's SHANTIES AND FOREBITTERS (London, 1914), Terry's SALT SEA BALLADS (London, 1931), and THE OXFORD SONG BOOK, published in two parts; Vol. 1 in 1916 and Vol. 2 in 1927. From the 1930s until I published my book SHANTIES

FROM THE SEVEN SEAS in 1961, there was a gap of many years in the publishing of shanty literature or music in Britain.

Four excellent books worth delving into are from the other side of the Atlantic, THE MINSTRELSY OF MAINE, by Fanny H. Eckstorm and Mary W. Smyth (Boston, 1927), THE BALLADS OF SEA SONGS OF NEW-FOUNDLAND, collected by Elizabeth B. Greenleaf and Grace Y. Mansfield (Harvard University Press, Cambridge, Mass., 1933), R. W. Mackenzie's BALLADS AND SEA SONGS FROM NOVA SCOTIA (Harvard University Press, Cambridge, Mass., 1928), and Helen Creighton's SONGS AND BALLADS FROM NOVA SCOTIA (Toronto, 1932).

Private collections of shanties, more difficult of access to the tyro, are those of J. M. Carpenter (some of which were published in the NEW YORK TIMES, 30 October 1938), Nathaniel Silsbee (in possession of Mrs George C. Beach of New York), Percy A. Grainger (hectograph copies in the Library of Congress, Washington, D.C.), and James H. Williams, who gave some of his shanties in THE INDEPENDENT (New York, 8 July 1909).

The most recently published collection of sailor songs is that of Gale Huntingdon. This is called SONGS THE WHALERS SANG and was published by the Barre Publishing Co. Inc., Barre, Mass., in 1964. Mr Huntingdon, a descendant of a long line of whaling men, read through hundreds of logbooks and journals kept by the old-time whalemen, and found in them many songs popular aboard the "blubber-butchers" of the eighteenth and nineteenth centuries. These songs he includes and annotates in his fine book, together with melody lines. Besides real whaling songs and forebitters from Merchant Service sources, there are, as to be expected, many shore folk-songs, music-hall and art-songs included in his pages.

For the student and folk-song singer who is interested in foreign shanties, and can understand the languages involved, there are several collections in German, French and Swedish. By far the best and most comprehensive German collection is Baltzer's KNURRHAHN. The original idea for this book was born in the winter of 1928-29 when the Kiel Canal was frozen over and the pilots, all sailing-ship men, formed a shanty group with Claus Prigge as their *Choremeister* (choirmaster). In 1939, Richard Baltzer put together in his book all the shanties these pilots sang. I have been told that the word *Knurrhahn* means "a fish that grunts" or "a cockerel with a sore throat"—alluding to the wild noises which were made by seamen when "singing-out". This first volume, which has a section devoted to English shanties, was later followed by a second volume, which was similar but printed in the picturesque Gothic style.

A shortened, post-war, paperback edition of this fine shanty book has been published by Hans Sikorski of Hamburg, and may be easier to obtain than earlier editions. Another German collection is ALTE SEEMANNSLIEDER UND SHANTIES, collected by Konrad Tegtmeier.

CHANSONS DE BORD is the collection of Capt. Armand Hayet, who claims to be the only man to have saved the real French deep-water shanty from oblivion—not the imitations he seems to think many of his confrères have collected. This book contains *chansons à virer* (capstan shanties), *chansons à hisser* (halyard shanties), *chansons à ramer* (rowing songs), and *chansons du gaillard d'avant* (forebitters). An even rarer volume, which he published under the pen name of Jean-Marie Le Bihor (Dunkirk, 1935), is called CHANSONS DE LA VOILE "SANS VOILES" (Songs of the Sail without Veils). This slim paperback volume is real sailor evidence as to how bawdy shanties really were. Another French collection, a mixture of respectable and bawdy, is CAHIER DE CHANSONS DE JEAN LOUIS POSTOLLEC ET DE JEAN LA PIPE. In 1918, Guy Arnoux published his CHANSONS DU MARIN FRANÇAIS, which, however, contains the type of material Capt. Hayet declares to be phoney.

Sweden has a wonderful collection of sea songs and shanties in SÅNG UNDER SEGEL, by Capt. Sigurd Sternvall, while Denmark has its INTERNATIONALE SØMANDS-OPSANGE, by Capt. Oscar Jensen. This latter also contains many English shanties. In Norway, a booklet called OPSANG FRA SEILSKIBSTIDEN was brought out by Capt. Diderik H. Brochmann in 1916. This contains much rare information about both Norwegian and English shanties.

The rather disturbing factor regarding all these above volumes, however, is their scarcity, and the interested singer and student may have to look long and hard before coming across copies.

On the aural side, shanty collections are as yet extremely inadequate. One of the first attempts to put shanties "on wax" was the series made by HMV in the mid-1920s with John Goss, baritone, as the shantyman, and the Cathedral Quartet as the "crowd". These records were certainly most successful in filling a long-felt need, but the manner of presenting them was more in keeping with that of the bold buccaneering baritone of Victorian times rolling forth *The Death Of Nelson*. Columbia, too, produced one or two records, but with ladies in the chorus; obviously out of keeping with the subject. A little later, Alan Mills and the "Shanty Men" made an LP disc for Folkways Records of New York, probably the largest number of shanties and sea-songs on any record—thirty-two to be exact—but Mills was once a confrère of Goss and I'm afraid a little of the latter's style has rubbed off on him. In our own country, the BBC and the English Folk Dance and Song Society recorded Stanley Slade, an old shantyman, performing five sailor shanties on the HMV label.

A few years rolled by, and the shanty was virtually unheard in the gramophone world until the Workers' Music Association came on the scene with their magnificent Topic LP disc *The Singing Sailor*, with A. L. Lloyd and Ewan MacColl as the shantymen. This was a more true-to-life performance than previous record performances. It included, I think for the first time on records, the forebitter. Following this, several other discs came on the market, some good, some too "arty". On the mainland of Europe too, the Kiel pilots of KNURRHAHN fame produced a disc called *Rolling Home*, and in France, Hayet's shanties (his cleaner ones) were presented on an LP disc.

In America, the tape recorder had been busy in Sailors' Snug Harbour, the results transferred to disc being eventually placed in the Library of Congress as part of the Archive of American Folk-song. Doerflinger's shantyman Dick Maitland sang several shanties for these two discs. In Britain, Peter Kennedy of the English Dance and Folk Society brought out a sea-song record called *A Pinch of Salt*, in HMV's Folk Music Series, and a few years later, in 1961, he roped in the writer to do fourteen shanties on an LP disc for the same series, with the York and Albany Folk-song Group as the "crowd". This record, like my book, is called *Shanties From the Seven Seas*. In recent years, Stan Kelly of Liverpool and Bob Roberts, master of the sailing barge *Cambria*, have each brought out EP discs of shanties and sea-songs. The most recent effort up to the time of writing is Topic's *Farewell Nancy*, which has five of Britain's most famous folk-song singers as shantymen.

However, as is fairly obvious, there is still room for the many hundreds of shanties and forebitters collected in the past to be recorded. The sailing ships and their tough salty seamen have departed, but we must not lose their glorious tradition of song. The printed page is not enough; songs have to be sung and heard.*

Folk-singers and others who are interested in the shanty must keep up a steady bombardment until the gramophone companies give them the necessary chance to keep alive the salt-water tradition of "Strike a light, there, shantyman!" And from the dais of many a folk-song club, young folk-singers must not keep to the well-worn and safe "oldies" but must set themselves the task of rendering the lesser-known shanties and forebitters that are at present a-mouldering in the shanty books.

* Since I wrote this a collection of sailor songs and shanties, sung by Ewan MacColl and A. L. Lloyd, called *A Sailor's Garland*, has been produced by Transatlantic Records Ltd, and two excellent L.P.s of whaling songs, recorded by the same singers and called *Whaler Out of New Bedford* and *Leviathan*, have been released by Folkways and Topic Records Ltd. respectively. Also Oak Records have Derek Sergeant singing four sea songs on an E.P. called *A Sailor's Life*.

THE SONGS

WE'RE ALL BOUND TO GO

This greatly liked windlass shanty came into being about the time of the Irish Potato Famine, when thousands of migrating Irish were passing through Liverpool heading for "Amerikee".

Tapscott was a well-known packet agent of Oldhall Street, Liverpool, and publisher of the famous TAPSCOTT'S EMIGRANT GUIDE. It is doubtful if his company had any hand in the low-down trick of leading emigrants to believe that the ship in which they were sailing was a fast mail packet and not a slow "wagon", merely down by the head with a meal for their bellies. This trick was common among lesser-known and more unscrupulous agents. An earlier song, from which the words of our present version may have stemmed, is *The Irish Emigrant* with its refrain of "Lay me down, lay me down, lay me down do!" Undoubtedly it is a song of Irish origin and seamen always sang it in imitative Irish brogue. In other shantymen's mouths the names of the ships concerned would be different, and in later days when the "meal" theme became outdated new sets of words were sung by the sailors. One version is that of "Where are ye goin' to my pretty maid?" a common set of unusually obscene words, sung to many other shanties at different times.

The Castle Garden was, in those days, a rather notorious piece of land which juts out into the junction of the East and Hudson Rivers, New York. On this piece of land was a shed, a sort of early Ellis Island set-up, in which the emigrants were incarcerated until they had satisfied the immigration authorities of their genuine desire to become American citizens.

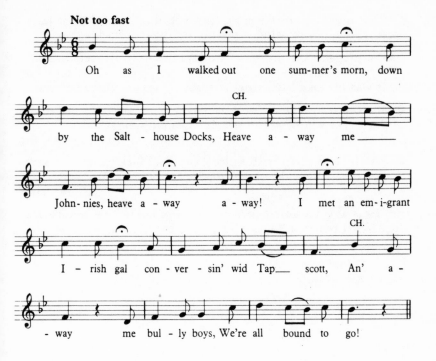

Not too fast

Oh as I walked out one sum-mer's morn, down by the Salt - house Docks, Heave a - way me ___ John- nies, heave a - way a - way! I met an em- i-grant I - rish gal con - ver - sin' wid Tap___ scott, An' a - way me bul - ly boys, We're all bound to go!

WE'RE ALL BOUND TO GO

1. Oh as I walked out one summer's morn, down by the
Salthouse Docks,
Ch. Heave away, me Johnnies, heave away—away!
I met an emigrant Irish gal conversin' wid Tapscott,
Ch. An' away, me bully boys, we're all bound to go!

2. "Good mornin', Mister Tapscott, sir." "Good morn, me
gal," sez he.
"Oh, it's have yiz got a packet ship, All bound for
Amerikee?"

3. "Oh, yes, I have got a packet ship, I have got one or two,
I've got the *Jinny Walker* an' I've got the *Kangaroo*.

4. "I've got the *Jinny Walker* and today she does set sail,
With five an' fifty emigrants an' a thousand bags o' meal."

5. The day was fine when we set sail but night had barely come,
An' every lubber never ceased to wish himself at home.

6. That night as we was sailin' through the Channel of St James,
   A dirty nor'west wind came up an' druv us back again.

7. We snugged her down an' we laid her to, with reefed main
                                                   tops'l set,
   It was no joke I tell you, 'cos our bunks an' clothes wuz wet.

8. It cleared up fine at break o' day, an' set sail once more,
   An' every son-o'-a-gun wuz glad when we reached
                                              Amerikee's shore.

9. Bad luck to them Irish sailor-boys, bad luck to them, I says,
   For they all got drunk, an' broke into me bunk, an' stole
                                              me clothes away.

10. 'Twas at the Castle Gardens, oh, they landed me ashore,
    An' if I marry a Yankee boy, I'll cross the seas no more.

SALLY BROWN

This windlass shanty probably came to life in the West Indies. Many variants exist, such as *Walkalong You Sally Brown, Roll, Boys, Roll* and *Hilo Johnny Brown*. In Jamaica as late as the 1930s *Sally Brown* helped logwood cutters to roll the logs down to the water's edge. The mysterious "Wild Goose Nation" appears in this song as it does in many other shanties but mainly in the general utility shanty *We'll Ranzo Way*. The location of this nation has been placed in West Africa, in the Southern States, in Ould Oirland, and I have had a bash at placing it somewhere close to New Bedford, Mass. Probably its origin will remain lost in the mists of Shantydom together with the origin of Sally Brown herself. Like Stormalong, the popular hero of many shanties and the embodiment of the perfect sailor, Sally Brown was more than likely the sailor's personification of all the girls of the ports of the world—a combination of sweetheart and harpy.

When the shantyman ran out of stanzas singing of Sally he usually got on to those singing of Sally's daughter, and on occasions these words, often obscene, were fitted to that beautiful capstan song *Shenandoah*, much to the disgust of some collectors who like to aver that Shenandoah was one of the shanties Jack Salt never defiled.

And when the job was a long one couplets from *Stormalong* too would be roped in by a competent shantyman.

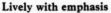

SALLY BROWN

1. Ooh! Sally Brown she's a bright mulatter,
   Ch. Way-ay, roll an' go!
   She drinks rum an' chaws terbacker,
   Ch. Spend my money on Sally Brown!

2. Sally lives on the ol' plantation,
   She is a daughter of the Wild Goose Nation,

3. Seven long years I courted Sally,
   But all she did was dilly-dally.

4. I bought her gowns an' I bought her laces,
   Took her out to all the places.

5. But Sally Brown she wouldn't marry,
   An' I no longer cared to tarry.

6. So I shipped away on a New Bedford whaler,
   When I got back she wuz courtin' a tailor.

7. An' so, me boys, I took a notion,
   To sail again the stormy ocean.

8. But now me troubles they are over,
   Sally's married to a nigger soger.

9. He beat her up an' stole her money,
   Then left her with a nigger baby.

10. Now, Sally Brown I love yer daughter,
   Give her rum without any water.

SANTIANA

Santiana, a windlass shanty, was extremely popular with Merchant Jack and was one of three work-songs roped in by whalemen to lighten their pulley-hauling. The other two songs popular aboard whalers were the halyard shanty *Ranzo* and the general-purpose shanty *We'll Ranzo Way*. Strangely enough, the whalers did not produce any shanties of their own.

The figure around whom this shanty is woven was Antonio Lopez de Santa Anna, who lived from 1795 to 1876 and was the last president of Mexico prior to the annexation of California, New Mexico and Texas by the United States of America. Defeating the Spaniards at Zampico, the French at Vera Cruz, and the Yankees at the Alamo, he was brought to a halt at Molina del Rey—the Molly de Rey of the shantymen—by the American troops under General Taylor. British sailors often deserted their ships during the Mexican War of 1846–48 in order to join Santiana's ragtag and bobtail army. For some strange reason—the rebel in them, no doubt—they favoured the Mexicans and not the Americans. This is probably the reason why most shantymen sang a lie: "Santiana gained the day . . . and General Taylor ran away." Santiana was recalled to the presidency in 1853 but finally overthrown in 1855.

When the last American whaler, the *Charles Morgan*, was being hauled into port for the last time, with her crowd at the windlass roaring out *Santiana*, it is reported that many old-timers on the quayside had tears in their eyes as they listened to the swelling choruses of this ancient work-song. There is a theory that this shanty antedates the Mexican War. Captain Bone wonders whether the Breton St Anne may have been the subject around whom this shanty was woven, and Dr John Lyman, the American nautical historian, working on a rather old version of *Santiana* found in a Danish shanty book, has wondered whether a Latin home may be found for it, since a vessel called the *Santa Anna* was known to have sailed the waters of the Mediterranean in the sixteenth century.

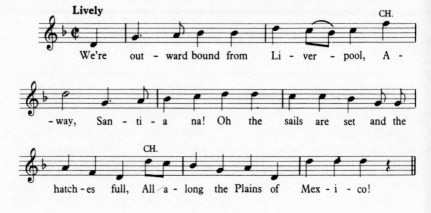

Lively

We're out-ward bound from Li - ver - pool, A-
-way, San - ti - a na! Oh the sails are set and the
hatch - es full, All a - long the Plains of Mex - i - co!

SANTIANA

1. We're outward bound from Liverpool,
   Ch. Away, Santiana!
Oh the sails are set and the hatches full,
   Ch. All along the plains of Mexico!

2. We're outward bound for Mexico,
To Mexico where the whalefish blow.

3. In Mexico where the land lies low,
Where there ain't no snow, an' the whalefish blow.

4. In Mexico so I've heard say,
There's many a charmin' señorita gay.

5. Them gals is fine with their long, black hair,
They'll rob yiz blind an' skin yiz bare.

6. Them Spanish gals I do adore,
They all drink vino an' ax for more.

7. In Mexico I long to be,
Wid a tight-waisted gal all on me knee.

8. Why do them yellar gals love me so,
Because I don't tell 'em all I know.

9. When I wuz a young man in me prime,
I'd chase them little gals two at a time.

10. But now I'm old an' getting grey,
Rum's me sweetheart every day.

128

11. Santiana gained his name,
    At Molly del Rey he gained his fame.

12. An' General Taylor ran away,
    An' Santiana gained the day.

13. 'Twas on the field at Molly del Rey,
    Santiana lost a leg that day.

14. So heave away for Mexico,
    For Mexico where them whalefish blow.

LOWLANDS

This song, used at both windlass and pumps, is one of the few in which Sailor John allowed a certain amount of tear-pulling material to be used. Normally, in his shanties anyway, he was averse to sentiment and tear-jerkers. It is quite possible that the general theme and wording of this shanty stemmed from some old border ballad of either Scottish or Geordie origin—the legend of drowned and seaweed-wrapped sweethearts, both male and female, returning in a dream being common in this part of the world. There exist several variants, all of a recitative type, and being rather difficult to sing, the song in general was only attempted by good shantymen. It was one of the shanties which passed through the Shanty Mart of the Gulf ports, turning up later with the final refrain rendered:

My dollar an' a half a day!

This was a shanty in which "stringing out" (repeating the solo lines to make the song last) was customary. A version in which the returning drowned lover is a male contains stanzas wherein the girl cuts her breasts until they bleed and stating that she will "cut away her bonnie hair" so that "no other man will think me fair". However, Sailor John would often level up this sentiment by singing:

She cut her hair, she cut her breasts,
Lowlands, away, my John!
Her hair was false, so was the rest,
My Lowlands away!

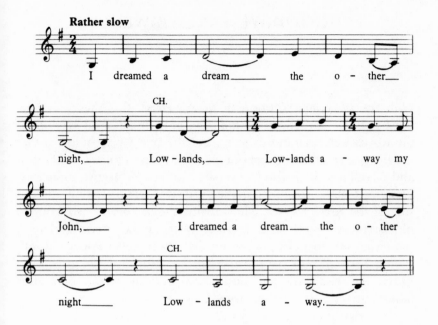

LOWLANDS

1. I dreamed a dream the other night,
   Ch. Lowlands, Lowlands away my John!
   I dreamed a dream the other night,
   Ch. Lowlands away!

2. I dreamed my love came in my sleep,
   Her cheeks were wet, her eyes did weep.

3. She came to me as my best bride,
   All dressed in white like some fair bride.

4. An' bravely in her bosom fair,
   A red, red rose did my love wear.

5. She made no sound, no word she said,
   An' then I knew my love was dead.

6. I bound the weeper round my head,
   For now I knew my love was dead.

7. An' then awoke to hear the cry,
   'Oh, watch on deck, oh, watch, ahoy!'

GOODBYE FARE-YE-WELL

With the possible exception of *Rolling Home*, this shanty was the most popular homeward-bound song of them all. Four versions of the words were commonly sung, but the one I give here was that usually preferred, by Liverpool seamen at least. Norwegian, French and German seamen also had versions in their respective languages. Wallasey Gates, mentioned in the third verse, are on the Birkenhead side of the River Mersey. The fourth verse has been lifted from an old forebitter *Outward and Homeward Bound*. Lime Street, Liverpool, is well known to most people and has always been associated with roving Tars with an eye for good grog-shops and bad girls. Even today, American seamen, both naval and merchant, make this famous street a port-o'-call when in Liverpool.

The singing of this shanty was probably heard at its best in the South American nitrate ports of Iquique, Antofogasta, Valparaiso and so on, when a homeward-bounder, loaded down to the gunnels with saltpetre, was about to heave her hook. The men from all the other ships in the mooring tiers would come aboard the homeward-bounder with a view to swelling the chorus. And that's exactly what did happen. The rising crescendos of the refrains would reverberate through the semi-circles of barren hills beneath which each of these ports nestles, causing great clouds of seabirds—gulls, shearwaters, gannets and boobies—to rise from their nests and join in the hurricane roar with wild caws and screams.

Oh, don't ___ yiz hear ___ the Old ___ Man

say? Good - bye fare - ye - well! good - bye fare - ye -

- well! Oh, don't yiz hear ___ the Old ___ Man

say? Hoo - raw me boys, we're home - ward bound!

GOODBYE FARE-YE-WELL

1. Oh, don't yiz hear the Old Man say?
   Ch. Goodbye fare-ye-well! goodbye fare-ye-well!
   Oh, don't yiz hear the Old Man say?
   Ch. Hooraw me boys, we're homeward bound!

2. We're homeward bound to Liverpool town,
   Where all them judies they will come down.

3. An' when we gits to the Wallasey Gates,
   Sally an' Polly for their flash men do wait.

4. An' one to the other ye'll hear them say,
   Here comes Johnny wid his fourteen months pay.

5. Them gals there on Lime Street we soon hope to meet,
   Soon we'll be a-rollin' both sides of the street.

6. We'll meet these fly judies an' we'll ring the ol' bell,
   With them judies we'll meet there, we'll raise merry hell.

7. I'll tell me ol' mammy when I gits back home,
   The gals there on Lime Street won't leave me alone.

8. We're homeward bound to the gals of the town,
   Then heave away, bullies, we're all homeward bound.

9. We're a fine, flashy packet an' bound for to go,
   Wid them gals on the towrope she cannot say no.

10. We're homeward bound, we'll have yiz to know,
    An' over the water to Liverpool must go.

LEAVE 'ER, JOHNNY, LEAVE 'ER

I have already mentioned that this shanty was the one sung on the last day of the voyage, although on some ships the men would prefer to sing *Only One More Day, Me Johnny*. However, when they sang *Leave 'er, Johnny, Leave 'er* as they tied the vessel up alongside or pumped her out for the last time, they would not sing the present version. Instead, they would air all their shipboard grievances in this song. The version we give here was sung at the pumps, and was more often used during the voyage, particularly aboard wooden ships, which needed pumping daily. This is a very old shanty, being based on two earlier forms: *Across the Rockies* and *Across the Western Ocean*. Both of these were heard aboard the first Western Ocean packet ships and were used at halyards as well as at the brake pumps. Norwegian and German versions are also known.

Oh,— heave a - way me bul - ly boys,

Leave 'er, John - ny, leave -'er! Oh, pump a - way an'

CH.

make some noise, Time for us ter leave 'er!

LEAVE 'ER, JOHNNY, LEAVE 'ER

1. Oh, heave away, me bully boys,
    Ch. Leave 'er, Johnny, Leave 'er!
  Oh, pump away an' make some noise,
    Ch. Time for us ter leave 'er!

2. Though times is hard, an' the wages low,
  There's a fathom o' water in the hold.

3. Oh, a dollar a day is a Jackshite's pay,
  To pump all night an' work all day.

4. The Ol' Man shouts, the pumps stand by,
  Oh, we can niver suck her dry.

5. Heave one more turn an' round she goes,
  Or each manjack will be kickin' up his toes.

6. It's pump or drown—the Ol' Man said,
  Or else damn soon ye'll all be dead.

7. Heave around or we shall drown,
  Hey, don't yiz feel her settlin' down?

8. Heave around them pump-bowls bright,
  There'll be no sleep for us this night.

9. The rats have gone, an' we the crew,
  It's time, me boys, that we went too.

10. Leave 'er, Johnny, we can pump no more,
  It's time we wuz upon dry shore.

PACKET SHIP

This brake-pump shanty relates the story of the famous mutiny of the *Bounty*. I have kept to the early shanty's form of the name of the Bounty's captain—Blight. Whether this is a misprint in the original collection or the way the sailors sang it we shall never know for certain. Modern historians may think the sailor tale a little too harrowing and an exaggeration, but my own feelings are that the hazing depicted in the shanty is fairly near the truth. As already stated, it is the last stanza that makes this shanty an interesting one from the point of view of age.

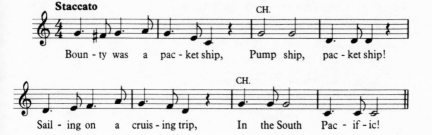

Boun - ty was a pac - ket ship, Pump ship, pac - ket ship!

Sail - ing on a cruis - ing trip, In the South Pac - if - ic!

PACKET SHIP

1. Bounty was a packet ship,
    Ch. Pump ship, packet ship!
  Sailing on a cruising trip,
    Ch. In the South Pacific!

2. Billy Blight, that silly man,
  Was the master in command.

3. He was growling day and night,
  Whether he was wrong or right.

4. On the *Bounty* were the rules,
  Not for soft an' silly fools.

5. An' the answer for complaints,
  Handcuffs an' the iron chains.

6. Spittin' on the quarterdeck,
  Punishment—a broken neck.

7. There was troubles every day,
  Many sailors ran away.

8. An' at last that Billy Blight,
  With his crew commenced to fight.

9. Brawling, kickin' everywhere,
  Iron pins flew through the air.

10. Mates an' sailors in the night,
  Overpowered Billy Blight.

11. They put Billy Blight afloat,
  With his madness, in a boat.

12. *Bounty* then went out of sight,
  Left alone was Billy Blight.

13. Billy Blight he reached the coast,
    But the *Bounty* she was lost.

14. Many gales have crossed the sea,
    Since the *Bounty* went away.

15. Never was there heard a word,
    From the crew that stayed on board.

YAW, YAW, YAW

The old-time sailing-ship John was always very partial to "furrin lingoes," although his knowledge of them was patchy. In this pumping song the sailor makes an attempt—a laughable one—at Dutch, or maybe German. A "Dutchman", in the lingo of the old-time sailorman, was any member of the Nordic race except that of Holland. The inhabitants of Holland he called "Holland Dutch". With this exception, as well as referring to anyone who said "ja" for yes as a Dutchman, he also called Scandinavians "Scandihoovians" or "Scowegians", and his generic term "Squarehead" covered, more or less, all these nationalities. He liked to imitate their tongues and was also rather partial to "ablaing" bad Spanish. All this, together with a smattering of pidgin English when in the China trade, and even some Hindustani, could be considered to be the complete linguistic ability of the average sailorman. However, I have known a few seamen who, during sojourns as beachcombers on the west coast of South America, managed to acquire a smattering of what they called "Quiché". I believe this to be an Indian tongue related to the speech of the ancient Incas. Another shanty in which the sailor imitated the "Holland Dutch" was:

Mein Vader vos ein Dutchman, ein Dutchman, ein Dutchman,
Mein vader vos ein Dutchman—Ach! Gott for dommey!
Heave away yer tops'l halyards, tops'l halyards, tops'l halyards,
Heave away yer tops'l halyards—the good ship lies low.

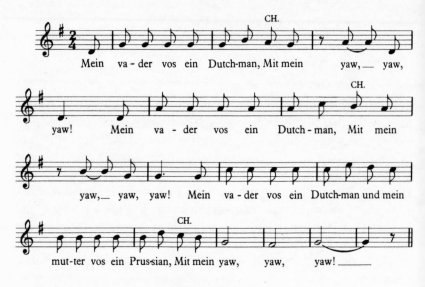

YAW, YAW, YAW

1. Mein vader vos ein Dutchman,
    Ch. Mit mein yaw, yaw, yaw!
Mein vader vos ein Dutchman,
    Ch. Mit mein yaw, yaw, yaw!
Mein vader vos ein Dutchman
Und mein mutter vos ein Prussian,
    Ch. Mit mein yaw, yaw, yaw!

2. Und I spoke ein hotch-potch lingo,
Und I spoke ein hotch-potch lingo,
Und I spoke ein hotch-hotch lingo,
Gott for Dommey und O by Yingo!

3. Mit mein niggerum, buggerum, stinkum,
Mit mein niggerum, buggerum, stinkum,
Vell, ve'll climb upon der steeples,
Und ve'll spit down on der peoples.

4. Und der polis-man, fireman, steepleman,
Und der polis-man, fireman, steepleman,
Dey all climb upon der steeple,
Und dey laugh do all der peoples.

5. Oh, ven I vos ein sailor,
Oh, ven I vos ein sailor,
Vell ve drink up all der whiskey,
Und it makes us feel damn frisky.

6. Ve did all de bawdy houses,
   Ve did all de bawdy houses,
   Und ve hitchum up der trousers,
   Und ve catchem all der louses.

7. Ve chase all der bretty frauleins,
   Ve chase all der bretty frauleins,
   Und ve chase um, und ve tease 'um,
   Und ve catch um, und ve kees 'um.

THE EBENEZER

Here we have a pumping song of Liverpool-Irish origin with an obviously Negro chorus. The song is one of those which at one time or other passed through the Shanty Mart of the Gulf ports of America. In its present form, however, its text points to a definite connection with the saltpetre ships which traded to the west coast of South America. Words like "geezer" show its Liverpudlian origin. A "Blackball cheeser" was a type of soft-crowned, peaked-cap—one without any stiffening in the crown. "Second greaser" is the Western Ocean packet-ship idiom for a second mate. "Molly-hawk" is a sailor mispronunciation for Mollymawk, a species of albatross frequently seen in the high latitudes and around Cape Horn.

Rather fast

I shipped on board of the *Eb - en - ez - er,*

Ev' - ry day 'twas scrub 'n' grease 'er, Send us a - loft to

scrape 'er down, An' if we growl they'll blow us down, Oh

git a - long boys, git a - long do, Han - dy me boys, so

han - dy! Git a - long boys, git a - long do,

Han - dy me boys, so han - dy!

THE EBENEZER

1. I shipped on board of the *Ebenezer,*
Every day 'twas scrub 'n' grease 'er,
Send us aloft to scrape 'er down,
An' if we growl they'll blow us down.

   Ch. Ooh! Git along, boys, git along do,
     Handy, me boys, so handy!
     Git along, boys, git along do,
     Handy, me boys, so handy!

2. The Ol' Man wuz a drunken geezer,
Couldn't sail the *Ebenezer;*
Learnt his trade on a Chinese junk,
Spent most time, sir, in his bunk.

143

3. The Chief Mate's name wuz Dickie Green, sir,
   The dirtiest bugger ye've ever seen, sir;
   Walkin' his poop wid a bucko roll,
   May the sharks have his body, an' the devil have his soul!

4. A Boston buck wuz second greaser,
   He used to ship in Limejuice ships, sir,
   The Limey packets got too hot,
   He jumped 'em, an' he cussed the lot.

5. The Bosun came from Tennessee, sir,
   He always wore a Blackball cheeser;
   He had a gal in every port,
   At least that's what his missus thought.

6. The *Ebenezer* wuz so old, sir,
   She knew Columbus as a boy, sir;
   'Twas pump 'er, bullies, night an' day,
   To help 'er git to Liverpool Bay.

7. Wet hash it wuz our only grub, sir,
   For breakfast, dinner an' for supper;
   Our bread wuz tough as any brass,
   An' the meat wuz as salt as Lot's wife's ass.

8. We sailed away before a breezer,
   Bound away for Vallaparaiser;
   Off the Horn she lost her sticks,
   The molly-hawks picked up the bits.

RIO GRANDE

Why the sailor sang of Rio Grande it is difficult to say. The port itself is situated on a "laguna", although "Rio Grande" means "Great River". In the old days, it was a real one-eyed port, its entrance a mass of shifting sandbanks; not a very attractive place at all. Perhaps it was the romantic sound of its name that caught the ear of the sailorman. Perhaps it was born during the days of the eighteenth-century gold rush, although I rather fancy the line found in some versions "It's there that the river runs down golden sands" describes the (one-time) huge sand dunes within the area rather than a prospector's dream. However, whatever the way of it, this capstan song was probably the most popular "outward-bounder" of them all. Whether a ship was actually bound to Rio, to pick up a cargo of coffee beans after discharging her saltfish, or bound to any one of the ports of the Seven Seas, this shanty would be one of the "hooraw choruses" raised by nine shantymen out of ten as the crowd trudged around the capstan-head. The singing of "away" was usually accompanied by a trilling sound. The expression "white-stockin' day" needs some explanation. Sailors of the present day still leave their half-pay or monthly allotment of pay to their wives, mothers and so on, just as sailors have done for generations. In the old days in Liverpool, when the womenfolk went to the shipping office to draw this half-pay, they would dress up in their "best bib and tucker" and don their long white cotton stockings, the hallmark of a lady of quality. They were determined to be ladies, if only for a day. The expression for this gathering of the "ladies" outside the shipping office was called "white-stocking day", and so durable are expressions emanating from the sea, ships and sailors, that it was still a current expression in Liverpool up till and during World War II, although I rather fancy it has since been drowned in a spate of Americanisms and post-war idioms.

With a swing

Oh, a ship went a-sai-lin' out o-ver the bar,

CH.

'Way___ for Ri-o!___They've poin-ted her bow to the

CH.

South-ern Star, An' we're bound for the Ri - o

FULL CHORUS

Grande!__Then a-waay, bul-lies, a-way!___

'Waay___ for Ri-o!___ Sing fare___ ye well___ me

Liv-er-pool gals, an' we're bound for the Ri - o Grande!

RIO GRANDE

1. Oh, a ship went a-sailin' out over the bar,
    Ch. 'Way for Rio!
They've pointed her bow to the Southern Star,
    Ch. An' we're bound for the Rio Grande!

    Full chorus. Then away, bullies, away!
        Away for Rio!
        Sing fare-ye-well, me Liverpool gels,
        An' we're bound for the Rio Grande!

2. Oh, say wuz ye niver down Rio Grande?
Them smart señoritas, they sure beats the band.

3. We wuz sick of the beach when our money wuz gone,
  So we signed in this packet to drive her along.

146

4. There's some of us sick, aye, there's some of us sore,
   We've scoffed all our whack an' we're looking for more.

5. Ye Parkee Lane judies we'll 'ave ye to know,
   We're bound to the south'ard, oh, Lord let us go!

6. Oh, pack up yer donkeys an' git under way,
   Them judies we're leavin' will git our half-pay.

7. Cheer up, Mary Ellen, now don't look so glum,
   On white-stockin' day ye'll be drinkin' hot rum.

8. We're a Liverpool ship wid a Liverpool crew,
   Ye can stick to the coast, but I'm damned if we do.

9. It's goodbye to Ellen an' sweet Molly, too,
   Ye Parkee Lane judies 'tis goodbye to you.

10. Heave only one pawl, then 'vast heaving, me sons,
    Sing only one chorus—it's blowin' big guns!

ROLLING HOME

Rolling Home competed with *Goodbye Fare-ye-well* in the homeward-bound popularity poll and, by English seamen, was usually chosen when the ship was leaving Australia; *Goodbye Fare-ye-well* being the favourite aboard homeward-bounders loaded with saltpetre from Chile or guano from Peru. Americans, in the main, preferred *Goodbye Fare-ye-well.* The tune of *Rolling Home* is an old Irish air, having been used at various times for rebel songs, the last song for which it was used being *Kevin Barry.* The usual set of words, not the ones we give here, are thought to have been composed by Charles Mackay on board ship in 1858. There are some people, however, who believe that Mackay heard sailors singing this song at the capstan, a song which he then trimmed and polished with his poetic pen.

The version we give here takes a ship from Australia to England. In the fourth verse "Heads" could be either Sydney Heads or Port Phillip Heads. In the eighth verse "Digger Ramrees" is the sailor name for a small and dangerous group of islands called Diego Ramirez. The "Western Islands" are the Azores, and the last line of the last verse means that from this point on the ship will be towed to her discharging port.

Not too fast

Call all hands to man the cap - s'n, See the ca - ble flaked down clear, Now we're sailin' home - ward bound boys, For the Chan - nel we will steer. Rol - lin' home, rol - lin' home, rol - lin' home a - cross the sea, Rol - lin' home to dear ol' Eng - land, Rol - lin' home, fair land to thee.

ROLLING HOME

1. Call all hands to man the caps'n,
   See the cable flaked down clear,
   Now we're sailin' homeward bound, boys,
   For the Channel we will steer.

   Ch. Rollin' home, rollin' home,
     Rollin' home across the sea,
     Rollin' home to dear ol' England,
     Rollin' home, fair land, to thee.

2. See yer tacks an' sheets all clear, boys,
   Lead down now yer buntlines all;
   Clear all gear upon the sheerpoles,
   Stand by to haul on the catfall.

149

3. Now Australia we are leavin',
   For old England give a cheer,
   Fare-ye-well, ye dark-eyed damsels,
   Give three cheers for English beer.

4. Goodbye, Heads, we're bound to leave you,
   Haul the towrope all inboard.
   We will leave old Aussie starnwards,
   Clap all sail we can afford.

5. Mister, set yer stuns'ls quickly,
   Set all flyin' kites ye can,
   Molly-hawks and chickens meet us,
   Souls of long-drowned sailor men.

6. Round Cape Horn on a winter's mornin',
   Now among the ice an' snow,
   Ye will hear our shellbacks singin',
   Sheet 'er home, boys, let 'er go!

7. Bullies, sweat yer weather braces,
   For the wind is strength'nin' now,
   Now we're roundin' Digger Ramrees,
   To the North our ship will plough.

8. Eighteen months away from England,
   Only fifty days, no more,
   On salt-horse an' crackerhash, boys,
   Boston beans that make us sore.

9. Now we're in the ol' Atlantic,
   With the royals no longer stowed,
   With our lee cathead a-divin',
   To the land—Lord let 'er go!

10. Now, we're low beneath the Islands,
    The lee riggin's hangin' slack,
    She's a-reelin' off her knots, boys,
    Hear the main t'gallant crack.

11. Now the Lizard Light's a-shinin',
    An' we're bound up to the Nore,
    With the canvas full an' drawin',
    Soon we'll be on England's shore.

12. Now we're passin' Dover Point, boys,
    Bullies, get yer cable clear,
    Give her thirty on the windlass,
    For the tugboat next we'll steer.

VALPARAISO ROUND THE HORN

This capstan song, considered a forebitter only by some authorities, started life in packet-ship days and, in our present form (with the old refrain "Raise tacks sheets an' mains'l haul!" changed to "We're bound for Vallaparaiser round the Horn!"), was well known aboard the saltpetre ships out of Liverpool to Chile's Flaming Coast. As a forebitter, the verses contain eight lines; when a shanty, these are divided into two four-liners. In the "saltpetre" form there are nineteen or twenty verses, which we have curtailed here, but which are to be found in my book SHANTIES FROM THE SEVEN SEAS (page 321). The repetitions, common to each line of verse and refrain, were known to every salt-water seaman, although, strangely enough, no existing shanty book apart from mine sets them out or even mentions them. In the seventh verse the line "But answered to the name of 'Month's Advance'" is a sailor quip on the fact that all these "furrin" members of the crew, not knowing a word of English but having been coached by the boarding-house masters to ask for a "month's advance", did just that when asked their names by the shipping master who was signing them on. The last verse indicates the prevalence of venereal disease among sailors in the old days, many of them carrying in their sea-chests "cures" that they had picked up from quacks all over the world.

With emphasis

'Twas a cold an' drea-ry mor-nin' in De-

-cem - ber (De-cem-ber), An' all of me mon-ey it wuz

spent (it wuz spent), Where it went to Lord I can't re-

-mem - ber (re-mem-ber), So - down to the Ship-pin' of - fice

went (went, went)___ CH. Pad-dy lay back, Pad-dy lay back!___

Take in yer slack, (take in yer slack!) Take__ a turn a-

(Shouted out)

-round yer cap - s'n, heave a pawl, heave a pawl!_____

_____ 'Bout ship, sta-tions, boys, be han - dy, be han-

-dy, For we're bound for Val - la - pa - rais - er round the Horn!

VALPARAISO ROUND THE HORN

1. 'Twas a cold an' dreary mornin' in December (December),
   An' all of me money it wuz spent (it wuz spent),
   Where it went to Lord I can't remember (remember),
   So down to the shippin' office went (went, went).

   Ch. Paddy, lay back, Paddy, lay back!
   Take in yer slack, take in yer slack!
   Take a turn around yer caps'n, heave a pawl, heave a
                           pawl!
   'Bout ship, stations, boys, be handy, be handy!
   For we're bound for Vallaparaiser round the Horn!

2. That day there wuz a great demand for sailors (for sailors),
   For the colonies and for 'Frisco and for France
                           (an' for France),
   So I shipped aboard a Limey barque the *Hotspur* (the *Hotspur*),
   An' got paralytic drunk on my advance ('vance, 'vance).

3. Now I joined 'er on a cold December mornin',
   A-frappin' o' me flippers to keep me warm,
   With the south cone a-hoisted as a warnin',
   To stand by the comin' of a storm.

4. Now some of our fellers had been drinkin',
   An' I meself wuz heavy on the booze;
   An' I sat upon me ol' sea-chest a-thinkin',
   I'd turn in me bunk an' have a snooze.

5. I woke up in the mornin' sick an' sore,
   An' knew I wuz outward bound again;
   When I heard a voice a-bawlin' at the door,
   "Lay aft, men, an' answer to yer names!"

6. 'Twas on the quarterdeck where first I saw 'em,
   Such an ugly bunch I'd niver seen before;
   For there wuz a bum an' stiff from every quarter,
   An' it made me poor ol' heart feel sick an' sore.

7. There wuz Spaniards an' Dutchmen an' Rooshians,
   An' Johnny Crapoos just across from France;
   An' most of 'em couldn't speak a word o' English,
   But answered to the name of "Month's Advance".

8. I wisht I wuz in the "Jolly Sailor",
   Along wid Irish Kate a-drinkin' beer;
   An' then I thought what jolly chaps were sailors,
   An' with me flipper I wiped away a tear.

9. I knew that in me box I had a bottle,
   By the boardin'-master 'twas put there;
   An' I wanted something for to wet me throttle,
   Somethin' for to drive away dull care.

10. So down upon me knees I went like thunder,
    Put me hand into the bottom of the box;
    An' what wuz my great surprise an' wonder,
    Found only a bottle of medicine for the pox.

SACRAMENTO

In the chapter on Historical Background, we have discussed the conditions under which this capstan song came into being. The similarity to Foster's *Camptown Races* is taken further in one version by the shantyman singing stanzas appropriate to this pseudo-Negro ditty:

> Went down thar wid mah hat caved in,
> Come back home wid mah pockets full o' tin,

and so on.

The gold rush of 1849 naturally brought to Frisco all kinds and conditions of men—and women. From Australia came ticket-o'-leave men, ex-Botany Bay convicts and bushrangers, and these were known collectively as the "Sydney Ducks". Such scum of the Colonies inhabited an area known as Sydney Town. When trouble arose people would remark "The Ducks are cacklin' in the pond tonight!" Frenchmen with dubious backgrounds flocked to Frisco and were nicknamed "Kiskadees" by the miners after a phrase in their lingo. Women of easy virtue came up from New Orleans and over from Paris as well, intent on fleecing the miners, but before they could take over they had to fight the already resident Chileno harlots who dwelt on the slopes of Telegraph Hill. Although the actual diggings were up on the Sacramento River it was Frisco that truly prospered from the work and wealth of the miners. And among all the mining and working, fighting and drinking, whoring and depravity, sailors were to be found by the thousand. A gold-field proverb ran: "Sailors, niggers and Dutchmen are the luckiest men in the mines; a very drunken old salt being the luckiest o' the lot!" Sailors were not only shanghaied out of the boarding-houses of the port when ships were swinging at their moorings devoid of crews, but sailors, the wiser ones, also took over as crimps, and as runners for the crimps, bar-keeps and brothel owners. In fact, when this shanty was attaining its greatest popularity, there were probably more sailors to be found ashore in Frisco than throughout the rest of the world at sea.

This capstan song was very well known to German seamen who sang it in Plaat Deutsch. Norwegians sang "Ota Hayti!" (a form of Captain Cook's Otaheite in the South Seas) for "hoodah" and Swedish tars sang "Oh, Bermudas, oh, Bermudas!" for the same refrain.

One Anglo-Saxon version was obscene to a degree, with the chorus also including a bawdy phrase.

O, a - round Cape Horn we are bound for to go, To me hoo - dah, To me hoo - dah! A - round Cape Horn thro' the sleet an' the snow, To me hoo - dah, hoo - dah day! Blow, boys,___ blow! for Ca - li - forn - eye - O! There's plen - ty o' gold so I've bin told, On the banks of the Sac - ra - men - to!

SACRAMENTO

1. O, around Cape Horn we are bound for to go,
  Ch. To me hoodah, to me hoodah!
Around Cape Horn thro' the sleet an' the snow,
  Ch. To me hoodah, hoodah day!

  Full Chorus. Blow, boys, blow!
        For Californ-eye-O!
        There's plenty of gold so I've bin told,
        On the banks of the Sacramento!

2. Oh, around Cape Horn in the month of May,
Oh, around Cape Horn is a bloody long way.

3. Oh, around Cape Horn wid a main-skys'l set,
Around Cape Stiff an' we're all wringin' wet.

4. To the Sacramento we're bound away,
For there the gold's more bright than day.

5. Round the Horn an' up to the Line,
We're the buckos for to make 'er shine.

6. We're the buckos for to make 'er go,
All the way to the Sacramento.

7. Breast yer bars an' bend yer backs,
Heave, an' make yer spare ribs crack.

8. Ninety days to Frisco Bay,
Ninety days fer to make our pay.

9. Them Spanish gals ain't got no combs,
They comb their hair wid tunny-fish bones.

10. Oh, them wuz the days o' the good ol' times,
Back in the days of the Forty-nine.

THE LIVERPOOL JUDIES

The phrase "The Towrope Girls" was a common one in the days of sail. When a ship was homeward bound with a favourable wind, someone would remark "Aye, the gals 'ave got 'old of our towrope, me hearties!" They were a sort of magnet, supposedly pulling the sailors and their ship towards the land. Sailors may have been crude, tending to express their animal instincts, but through all their roughness and toughness would shine, at times, brilliant flashes of poetry. In the case of this shanty, the common Liverpool word for a young girl was used—"Judy". There are two regular patterns to this shanty, the one we give, and one which tells of a sailor missing his ship in Frisco and getting shanghaied aboard another, and of his passage around Cape Horn to the Bramley Moore Dock, Liverpool. The version we give is also a shanghaiing one, but in this case it is out of New York.

In the 1840s, when this shanty probably came into being, New York's Sailortown was notorious for its crimps and boarding-house masters, only outdone in infamy by San Francisco's Barbary Coast. One of its most infamous boarding-house-cum-saloons was the "Hole-in-the-Wall" run by a tough boarding mistress called Gallus Meg. She was her own bouncer, and after having a rough-house with an obstreperous seaman she would cut off one of his ears and place it in a jar of methylated spirits. A whole row of these grisly mementoes of her fights adorned a shelf behind the bar. Other dealers in sailor flesh were Martin Churchill of Cherry Street, Joe Brennan and Mother Fairvelt. They would dope sailors, clerks, parsons, cowhands, fakirs and shoemakers and, with equal speed, ship them aboard a Yankee hell-ship.

An alternative form of the chorus of this song gives, "Row, bullies, row!" Some think that these words suggest that, at some time or other, this shanty may have been a rowing song used aboard whalers, but of this we have no actual proof.

With a swing

When I wuz a young-ster I sailed wid de rest, On a Liv-er-pool pac-ket bound out to the West, We anchor-ed one day in de har-bour of Cork, Then we put out to sea for the port of New York, Singin' ro - o - o -oll, ro - o - o -oll, roll, bul – lies, roll! Them Liv-er-pool ju - dies have got us in tow!

CH.

THE LIVERPOOL JUDIES

1. When I wuz a youngster I sailed wid de rest,
On a Liverpool packet bound out to the West,
We anchored one day in de harbour of Cork,
Then we put out to sea for the port of New York.
   Ch. Singin' ro-o-o-oll, ro-o-o-oll, roll, bullies, roll!
   Them Liverpool judies have got us in tow!

2. For forty-two days we wuz hungry an' sore,
Oh, the winds wuz agin us, the gales they did roar;
Off Battery Point we did anchor at last,
Wid our jibboom hove in an' the canvas all fast.

3. De boardin'-house masters wuz off in a trice,
A-shoutin' an' promisin' all that wuz nice;
An' one fat ol' crimp he got cotton'd to me,
Sez he, "Yer a fool lad, ter follow the sea."

4. Sez he, "There's a job as is waitin' fer you,
   Wid lashin's o' liquor an' beggar-all to do;"
   Sez he, "What d'yer say, lad, will ye jump 'er, too?"
   Sez I, "Ye ol' bastard, I'm damned if I do."

5. But de best ov intentions dey niver gits far,
   After forty-two days at the door of a bar,
   I tossed off me liquor an' what d'yer think?
   Why the lousy ol' bastard 'ad drugs in me drink.

6. Now, the next I remembers I woke in de morn,
   On a three-skys'l yarder bound south round Cape Horn;
   Wid an' ol' suit of oilskins an' three pairs o' sox,
   An' a bloomin' big head an' a dose of the pox.

7. Now all ye young sailors take a warnin' by me,
   Keep a watch on yer drinks when the liquor is free,
   An' pay no attintion to runner or whore,
   Or yer head'll be thick an' yer fid'll be sore.

THE LIVERPOOL PACKET

There are several tunes to this capstan song, that of *Villikins* being adopted by some shantymen. It was a forebitter also, but in this case there would be no "coal-box" (chorus), and the ship concerned is named the *Dreadnaught*, nicknamed the "Bloodboat of the Atlantic". In the song, the ship follows the route normally taken by the packets across the Western Ocean—leaving the Salthouse Dock, Liverpool, sailing out past the Rock Light, down the Irish Sea, across the Atlantic, over the Banks of Newfoundland and into New York. An older and naval version of this song, mentioned elsewhere, is *The Flash Frigate* or *La Pique*.

At the Liv - er - pool Docks at the break o' the
day, I saw a flash pac - ket bound west - 'ard a-
-way, She was bound to the west - 'ard, Where the
wild wa - ters flow, She's a Liv - er - pool pac - ket, oh,
Lord let 'er go! Bound a - way - ay! Bound a-
-way - ay! Thro' the ice, sleet an' snow, She's a
Liv - er - pool pac - ket, oh, Lord let 'er go!

THE LIVERPOOL PACKET

1. At the Liverpool Docks at the break o' the day,
   I saw a flash packet bound west'ard away,
   She was bound to the west'ard, where the wild waters flow,
       Ch. She's a Liverpool packet, oh, Lord let 'er go!

    Full Chorus. Bound away! Bound away!
              Through the ice, sleet an' snow,
              She's a Liverpool packet,
              Oh, Lord let 'er go!

2. Oh, the time o' her sailin' is now drawin' nigh,
   Stand by all ye lubbers we'll wish ye goodbye;
   A pair o' clean heels to ye now we will show,
       Ch. She's a Liverpool packet, oh, Lord let 'er go!

3. An' now we are leavin' the sweet Salthouse Docks,
   All the boys an' the gals on the pierhead do flock;
   All the boys an' the gals are all shoutin' hurro!
       Ch. She's a Liverpool packet, oh, Lord let 'er go!

4. An' now we are waitin' in the Mersey so free,
   Awaitin' the tugboat to tow us to sea;
   An' we'll round the Rock Light where the salt tides do flow,
       Ch. She's a Liverpool packet, oh, Lord let 'er go!

5. Sheet home yer big tops'ls, haul aft yer jib sheets,
   Sheet home fore 'n' aft, boys, ye'll git no darn sleep;
   Come aft now, God damn yers, come aft, make a show,
       Ch. She's a Liverpool packet, oh, Lord let 'er go!

6. An' now we are howlin' down the wild Irish sea,
   Our passengers are merry an' their hearts full o' glee;
   Our sailors like tigers they walk to an' fro,
       Ch. She's a Liverpool packet, oh, Lord let 'er go!

7. An' now we are sailin' the Atlantic so wide,
   An' the hands are now ordered to scrub the ship's side;
   Now then, holystones, boyos, the bosun do blow,
       Ch. She's a Liverpool packet, oh, Lord let 'er go!

8. An' now we are off of the Banks o' Newf'n'land,
   Where the bottom's all fishes an' fine yellar sand;
   An' the fishes they sing as they swim to an' fro,
       Ch. She's a Liverpool packet, oh, Lord let 'er go!

9. An' now we're arrivin' in ol' New York town,
   We're bound for the Bowery, an' let sorrow drown;
   With our gals an' our beer, boys, oh, let the song flow,
       Ch. She's a Liverpool packet, oh, Lord let 'er go!

STRIKE THE BELL

The tune of this pumping shanty has been used throughout the world by the folk, on land and at sea. My father would sing a song called *Ring the Bell Watchman* which I believe is of Scottish origin and has the same air. In the shearing sheds down under, in Australia, *Click Go the Shears* uses the same tune. Wales claims what is probably the oldest song sung to this air, the song in question being called *Twll Bach y Clo*. The only difference is that this Welsh song has no chorus. However, I rather fancy that this sailor shanty has a claim as good as any in the age stakes. Even German and Scandinavian seamen sang it at the pumps, to English words. Somehow or other I overlooked this shanty in my SHANTIES FROM THE SEVEN SEAS, although I did print it in the folk-song magazine SPIN.

To get the hang of this song one must know something about the shipboard method of keeping time by means of bells. Incidentally, at sea, a bell is always "struck" never "rung". The twenty-four hours of a nautical day are divided into six watches of four hours each, commencing at midnight. Midnight is eight bells, 12.30 a.m. one bell, 1 a.m. two bells, 1.30 a.m. three bells, 2.0 a.m. four bells, 2.30 a.m. five bells, 3 a.m. six bells, 3.30 a.m. seven bells, and 4 a.m. eight bells and the end of the watch. Then one bell is struck again for 4.30 a.m. This was once the regular procedure for each four-hour watch, and in ships from the mainland of Europe and from America it still is, but in British ships, thanks to the Mutiny of the Nore, the watch from 4 p.m. to 8 p.m. is divided into two periods of two hours each called "dog-watches". The bells in the first dog-watch are struck in the usual order until 6 p.m. (four bells), then 6.30, the first half-hour of the second dog-watch, is given one bell only, with 7 p.m. having two bells, 7.30 p.m. three bells and 8 p.m. the usual eight bells. The reason for this breaking of the sequence is that at the Mutiny of the Nore the signal for the crews of all the naval ships concerned to down tools was the striking of five bells (originally 6.30 p.m.). After the revolt had been quelled, My Lords of the Admiralty had the bells changed to commemorate this major mutiny in the Royal Navy.

In sailing-ship days, the crews of merchant ships were divided into two watches—port and starboard. When the starboard watch were working on deck for four hours, the port watch would be asleep below. In the case of "All hands!" both the watch on deck and the watch below would be needed. There is one difference between the naval and Merchant Service way of striking the bell. This is when, at a quarter to 12, 4 and 8 a.m. and a quarter to 12, 4, and 8 p.m. in merchant ships, one bell is struck as a warning for the watch below to stand by to relieve the watch on deck.

Aft on the poop___ deck, walk - in' a - bout,

There is the se - cond mate, so stead - y an' so stout;

What he is think - in' of he does - n't know him - sel', O, we

wish that he would hur - ry up an' strike, strike the bell.

CH.

Strike th' bell, se - cond mate! Let us go be - low,

Look well to wind - 'ard, ye can see it's gonna blow,

Look at the glass, ye will see it has fell, An' we

wish that ye would hur - ry up an' strike, strike the bell!

STRIKE THE BELL

1. Aft on the poop deck, walkin' about,
   There is the second mate, so steady an' so stout;
   What he is thinkin' of he doesn't know himsel',
   O, we wish that he would hurry up an' strike, strike the bell.

   Ch. Strike the bell, second mate! Let us go below,
      Look well to wind'ard, ye can see it's gonna blow,
      Look at the glass, ye will see it has fell,
      An' we wish that you would hurry up an' strike, strike the
                                                                bell!

2. Down on the maindeck workin' at the pumps,
   There is the larboard watch a-longin' for their bunks;
   Lookin' to wind'ard they see a great swell,
   They're wishin' that the second mate would strike, strike the
                                                                bell.

3. Aft at the wheel poor Anderson stands,
   Grasping at the spokes wid his cold, mittened hands;
   Lookin' at the compass, oh, the course is clear as hell,
   He's wishin' that the second mate would strike, strike the bell.

4. For'ard on the fo'c'slehead keeping sharp lookout,
   There is Johnny standin', ready for to shout,
   "Lights burnin' bright, sir, an' everything is well!"
   He's wishin' that the second mate would strike, strike the bell.

5. Aft on the quarterdeck our gallant captain stands,
   Lookin' to wind'ard, his glasses in his hands;
   What he is thinkin' of we know very well,
   He's thinkin' more of shortening sail than strike, strike the
                                                                bell!

A-ROVIN'

Many authorities believe *A-rovin'* to be a shanty of great age and, originally, a shore-song. Unfortunately, we have no proof of these statements which are based on the words of the song only. The words, such theorists say, were taken from a catch, found in Thomas Heywood's comedy *The Rape of Lucrece* (1640). This song, like many used by Elizabethan and later dramatists in their plays, savours of the bawdy, and is one which could be called an "anatomical progression" song. *A-rovin'*, in its raw state, is certainly bawdy, so is *Gently Johnny my Jingalo* and the more modern *Roll Me Over in the Clover*, and this song of Heywood's is probably the sire of them all; but beyond this, I doubt if it has any real connection with *A-rovin'*. The air and its variants have been found in the Low Countries also, but as a shanty I do not believe it to be much older than others of its ilk.

The story leading up to the song, as found in Heywood's *The Rape of Lucrece*, tells of a Clowne who had visited Italy and been the observer of certain indiscretions commited by Lucrece and a man called Sextus. Back in England, Valerius and Horatius want the Clowne to tell them what happened: "Speake what did Sextus there with thy faire mistresse?" But the Clowne wouldn't tell them. Then Valerius says: "Second me my Lord, and weale vrge him to disclose it." But the Clowne still refuses to tell them. They then prevail upon him to sing about the incident.[1]

---

[1] This is an incident fairly comparable to the origin of a certain sailor song in which a sailor who stutters is on the tops'l yard. He shouts unintelligibly to the mate below that his "whatnots" are jammed in the block of the reefing tackle. The mate responds by bawling aloft: "If yer can't speak it, me bucko, sing it!" And the sailor returns, musically, with:

> Slack away yer reefy tackle, reefy tackle, reefy tackle,
> Slack away yer reefy tackle, me whatnots are jammed!

It is common knowledge that most people who stutter, when singing do not.

Here is the song:

Val. Did he take faire Lucrece by the toe man?
Clow. Toe man.
Val. I man.
Clow. Ha ha ha ha ha man.
Hor. And further did he striue to go man?
Clow. Goe man.
Hor. I man.
Clow. Ha ha ha ha man, fa derry derry downe a ha fa derry dino.
Val. Did he take faire Lucrece by the heele man?
Clow. Heele man.
Val. I man.
Clow. Ha ha ha ha ha man.
Hor. And did he further striue to feele man?
Clow. Feele man.
Hor. I man.
Clow. Ha ha ha man, ha fa derry, *etc.*
Val. Did he take the Lady by the shin man?
Clow. Shin man.
Val. I man.
Clow. Ha ha ha ha ha man.
Hor. Further too would he haue bene man?
Clow. Bin man.
Hor. I man.
Clow. Ha ha ha ha ha man. Ha fa derry, *etc.*
Val. Did he take the Lady by the knee man?
Clow. Knee man.
Val. I man.
Clow. Ha ha ha ha man.
Hor. Further then that would he be man?
Clow. Be man.
Hor. I man.
Clow. Ha ha ha ha man, hey fa derry, *etc.*
Val. Did he take the Lady by the thigh man?
Clow. Thigh man.
Val. I man.
Clow. Ha ha ha ha man.
Hor. And now he came it some what nye man.
Clow. Nie man.
Val. But did he doe the tother thing man?
Clow. Thing man?
Val. I man.
Clow. Ha ha ha ha man.
Hor. And at the same had he a fling man.
Clow. Fling man.
Hor. I man.
Clow. Hay ha ha ha man, hey fa derry, *etc.*

Not too fast

In Am-ster-dam— there lived— a— maid, Mark well what I do say! In Am-ster-dam there lived— a— maid, an' she wuz mis-tress— of her trade, We'll go no more a-rov-in'—with you fair maid. A-rov-in', a-rov-in' since rov-in's bin me— ru-eye-in, We'll go no more a-ro-oo-vin'—with you fair maid.

A-ROVIN'

1. In Amsterdam there lived a maid.
  Ch. Mark well what I do say!
In Amsterdam there lived a maid,
An' she wuz mistress of her trade.
  Ch. We'll go no more a-rovin' with you fair maid!

Full Chorus. A-rovin', a-rovin',
      Since rovin's bin me ru-eye-in,
      We'll go no more a-rovin',
      Wid you fair maid.

2. One night I crept from my abode,
To meet this fair maid down the road,

3. I met this fair maid after dark,
She took me to her favourite park.

4. I took this fair maid for a walk,
   An' we had such a lovin' talk.

5. I put me arm around her waist,
   Sez she, "Young man yer in great haste!"

6. I put me hand upon her knee,
   Sez she, "Young man yer rather free!"

7. I put me hand upon her breast,
   Sez she, "The wind is veerin' sou'-sou'-west!"

8. "The wind is veerin' sou'-sou'-west,"
   Her voice was as deep as an ol' sea-chest.

9. The cheeks of her ass wuz as tight as a drum,
   The lips o' her mouth wuz as red as a plum.

10. Her skin wuz as white an' as creamy as milk,
    The hair o' her legs wuz as soft as silk.

11. I put me hand upon her thigh,
    Sez she, "Young man yer rather high!"

12. I pushed her over on her back,
    An' then she let me have me whack.

13. In three weeks' time I wuz badly bent,
    Then off to sea I sadly went.

14. In a Yankee bloodboat round Cape Horn,
    Me boots 'n' clothes wuz all in pawn.

15. An' then back to the Liverpool Docks,
    Saltpetre stowed in me boots and sox.

16. Now when I got back home from sea,
    A soger had her dancin' on his knee!

THE BOSUN'S ALPHABET

This pumping song and forebitter is of fair age, possibly being known in the mid-eighteenth century. Shore forms have been found in Britain based on various trades, and in America both *The Lumberman's Alphabet* and a very early form of *The Sailor's Alphabet* are well known. *The Sailor's Alphabet* has for the letter "U" the word "Union", the union of England and Scotland. This is one possible clue to its age. Of the Nautical terms used in the shanty, several need explaining.

In the second verse, "Earring" is a rope used in reefing (shortening the area of a sail when the wind becomes too strong). After the reef-band or temporary "head" of the sail has been hauled up to the yard by means of the reef tackles, a rope called an "earing" is passed through the reef-cringle and through an eyebolt on the end of the yard in order to keep the new "corner" of the sail to the yard-arm. This is done at both sides of the squaresail. In the third verse, "Knightheads" are huge baulks of oak positioned upright well for'ard on the fo'c'slehead, between which the heel (the inboard end of the bowsprit) is wedged. The knightheads was a favourite place for the shantyman to stand while the men were heaving around the capstan. The "Orlop" deck mentioned in the fourth verse was a 'tween-deck of the old wooden walls rather than of merchant ships. The "Peter" referred to in the same verse is, of course, the Blue Peter, the flag flown on sailing day. The term possibly comes from a flag of similar design in Nelson's signal code—the Blue Repeater; or it might be the anglicized French word *partir*, meaning "to leave". In the fifth verse, the "Quadrant", in its simplest form, was an arc of metal at the inboard head of the rudder, to which the steering-chains running from the steering wheel were shackled. The "Sheerpole" mentioned in this verse was a spar of wood in the rigging, above the top deadeye blocks, positioned in line with the "sheer" (curve) of the ship's deck. "Topmen", also in the fifth verse, is a naval expression for men whose job it was to see to all work in the upper rigging. In fact, these men virtually lived in the "tops". The most famous topman in literature is Billy Budd, in Herman

Melville's book of that name. "Vangs", in the sixth verse, are two steadying guys running down to the deck from the end of a gaff, usually found on a spanker or spencersail. The "Stormy" referred to in the same verse is that personification of all good sailormen, Old Stormalong.

THE BOSUN'S ALPHABET

1. A is for the Anchor that lies at our bow,
   B is for the Bowsprit an' the jibs all lie low,
   Oh! C is for the Caps'n we all run around,
   D is for the Davits to low'r the boat down.

   Ch. Sooo! merrily, so merrily, so merrily sail we,
   There's no mortal on earth like a sailor at sea,
   Blow high or blow low! as the ship sails along,
   Give a sailor his grog an' there's nothing goes wrong!

2. E is for the Earring when reefing we haul,
   F is for the Fo'c'sle where the bullies do brawl,
   Oh! G is for the Galley where the saltjunk smells strong,
   H is for the Halyards we hoist with a song.

3. I is for the Eyebolt—no good for the feet,
   J is for the Jibs, boys, stand by the lee sheet,
   Oh! K is for the Knightheads where the shantyman stands,
   L is for the Leeside hard found by new hands.

4. M is for the Maindeck—as white as new snow,
   N is for the Nigger gals in the land to which we go,
   Oh! O is for the Orlop, 'neath the 'tweendecks it lays,
   P is for the Peter flown on sailin' day.

5. Q is for the Quadrant—to the wheel it lies near,
   R is for the Rudder—it helps us to steer,
   Oh! S is for the Sheerpole over which we must climb,
   T is for the Topmen, 'way aloft every time.

6. U is for Uniform—only worn aft,
   V is for the Vangs running from the main gaff,
   Oh! W is for the Water—we're on pint and pound,
   X marks the Spot where Ol' Stormy wuz drowned.

7. Y is for Yard-arm—needs a good sailorman,
   Z is for Zoe—I'm her fancy-man,
   So this is the end of me bully ol' song,
   Heave away, buckos, oh, heave long an' strong!

RANZO

Always a very popular hauling song at tops'l halyards, *Ranzo* was also one of the few shanties used aboard whalers. Many theories have been put forward as to who was the original Ranzo—a Polish Jew, a Cape Verde Islander, even a Danish hero. My own opinion, however, is that he was a Sicilian or Italian fisherman. He may have shipped aboard a salt-carrier from Trapani, in Sicily, to the States. Then, aboard some Yankee hell-ship, the sailors appropriated a fisherman's song he used to sing, basing its Anglo-Saxon theme on the hellish hazing he had to suffer owing to his inadequate knowledge of deep-water seamanship and to his Latin habits. They then used a shortened form of his name—possibly Lorenzo—for the lethal refrains. A song which I believe he may have sung helped me to form this theory—a theory as good as and probably much better than most. This song is a Sicilian fisherman's song sung when hauling in the nets of tuna. Its tune is identical with that of our *Ranzo*, and the words of the first verse (the places where the pulls came are italicised) are as follows:

> 'Sciucamunni 'sta lampa!
> *Lamp*abbo! *Lamp*a!
> Di cca nun si ni jèmu!
> *Lamp*abbò! *Lamp*a![1]

[1] Put out the lamp, boys,
  From here we'll not be moving.
"Put out the lamp" is equivalent to the toast of 'Bottoms up!'".

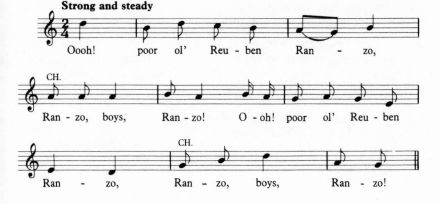

Strong and steady

Oooh! poor ol' Reu - ben Ran - zo,

CH.

Ran - zo, boys, Ran - zo! O - oh! poor ol' Reu - ben

CH.

Ran - zo, Ran - zo, boys, Ran - zo!

RANZO

1. Oooh! poor ol' Reuben Ranzo,
  Ch. Ranzo, boys, Ranzo!
Oooh! poor ol' Reuben Ranzo,
  Ch. Ranzo, boys, Ranzo!

2. O, Ranzo wuz no sailor,
He wuz a New York tailor.

3. Though Ranzo wuz no sailor,
He shipped aboard of a whaler.

4. Ranzo couldn't steer 'er,
Did ye ever hear anything queerer.

5. The mate he wuz a dandy,
Far too fond of brandy.

6. They put him holystonin',
An' cared not for his groanin'.

7. They said he wuz a lubber,
An' made him eat whale-blubber.

8. He washed once in a fortnight,
He said it wuz his birthright.

9. They took him to the gangway,
An' gave him lashin's twenty.

10. They gave him lashes thirty,
Because he wuz so dirty.

11. The Capen gave him thirty,
His daughter begged for mercy.

12. She gave him cake an' water,
    An' a bit more than she outer.

13. She taught him navigation,
    An' gave him eddication.

14. Ranzo now is skipper,
    Of a Yankee whaler.

15. He married the Ol' Man's daughter,
    An' still sails on blue water.

16. He's known wherever them whalefish blow,
    As the toughest bastard on the go.

BLOW THE MAN DOWN

This was the classic tops'l-halyard shanty of the Western Ocean Packet Rats. Several versions exist, probably the most popular with the sailor being the one in which he chases a "flash packet" up Paradise Street in the sailor quarter of Liverpool. But the one we give here, in which he gets into a contretemps with a Liverpool scuffer (policeman) in the same street, was equally popular. This version dates from the time when Dutchmen and other "square-heads" were entering the British and Yankee merchant fleets. The Packet Rats naturally took umbrage at these intruders in their pre-serves, and showed their dislike by robbing "them damn yaw-yaw men" and worrying them in many ways. The waterfront policeman is aware of this custom and when he sees the sailorman in new-looking gear jumps to the conclusion that he's bilked some Dutchman of it. The sailor protests that he is not a "Blackballer" but a sailor from a ship on the Far Eastern run—a "flying fish sailor" being a tea-clipper sailorman. This version appears to be based on a Scottish folk-song *Erin-go-Bragh*. Sometimes, to all the versions, an introductory verse would be sung by the shantyman:

> I'm a flying fish sailor, just home from Hong Kong,
> If ye'll give me some whiskey I'll sing ye a song.

Or:

> I'll sing ye a song all about the high sea,
> An' I'll trust that ye'll join in this chorus wid me.

Rolling and not too fast

Oh, as I wuz a - rol - lin' down Pa - ra - dise
Street, Tim me way, hay, blow the man down! A
fat I - rish bob - by I chanct for to meet, Ooh!
gim - me some - time to blow the man down!

BLOW THE MAN DOWN

1. Oh, as I wuz a-rollin' down Paradise Street,
    Ch. Timme way, hay, blow the man down!
  A fat Irish bobby I chanct for to meet,
    Ch. Ooh! gimme some time to blow the man down!

2. Sez he, "Yer a Blackballer by the cut o' yer hair,
  An' the long red-topped seaboots that I see you wear!"

3. "Ye've sailed in some packet that flies the Blackball,
  Ye've robbed some poor Dutchman of boots, clothes an' all."

4. "O mister, O mister, ye do me great wrong,
  I'm a flying fish sailor just home from Hong Kong."

5. So I spat in his face, an' I stove in his jaw,
  Sez he, "Young fellar, yer breakin' the law!"

6. They gave me six months, boys, in Liverpool town,
  For bootin' an' kickin' an' blowin' him down.

7. Now all ye young fellars what follows the sea,
  Put yer vents on the wind an' just listen to me.

8. I'll give ye a warnin' afore we belay,
  Steer clear o' fat policemen, ye'll find it'll pay.

9. Wid a blow the man up, bullies, blow the man down,
  An' a crew of hardcases from Liverpool town.

BLOW, BOYS, BLOW

The earliest version of this halyard shanty evolved in the latter days of the Guinea slave trade, roughly about the end of the eighteenth and the beginning of the nineteenth centuries. The "Embargo" mentioned in the song was that put upon the slave-traders by America and Britain, but many slave-ships were to be found dodging British and American men-o'-war long after the embargo became operative.

In later days, the Western Ocean packet seamen put their words to it, as did the hazed seamen of the hard-driving Yankee Cape Horners. The version we give here starts as did the old Guinea version, and then has some of the typical verses voiced by the crews of hell-ships. The names of the masters and mates of this ship were innumerable and many very "choice". The food mentioned also varied according to different shantymen. One version is rather comical, a sort of British satire on Yankee hell-ships. The line about the "masts and yards they shine like silver" sings of the terrible discipline and belayin'-pin authority of the bucko mates in the Yankee packets, and the working aloft on moonlit nights with sand and canvas in order to get the masts and yards "like silver".

This shanty was one of the unholy trinity of work-songs of the days of bucko mates and shanghaied crews—the other two being *Blow the Man Down* and the *Blackball Line*.

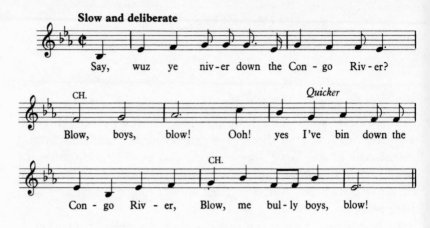

Slow and deliberate

Say, wuz ye niv-er down the Con - go Riv - er?

CH.

Quicker

Blow, boys, blow! Ooh! yes I've bin down the

CH.

Con - go Riv - er, Blow, me bul - ly boys, blow!

BLOW, BOYS, BLOW

1. Say, wuz ye niver down the Congo River?
    Ch. Blow, boys, blow!
Ooh! yes I've bin down the Congo River,
    Ch. Blow, me bully boys, blow!

2. Congo she's a mighty river,
Where the fever makes the White Man shiver,

3. A Yankee ship came down the river,
Her masts an' yards they shine like silver.

4. How d'yer know she's a Yankee clipper?
By the blood 'n' guts that flow from her scuppers.

5. How d'yer know she's a Yankee liner?
By the stars an' bars that fly behind her.

6. How d'yer know she's a Yankee packet?
She fired her guns an' I heard the racket.

7. Who d'yer think's the skipper of her?
A bow-legged bastard from the Bowery.

8. Who d'yer think's the chief mate of her?
Why Pompey Squash, that big, buck nigger.

9. What d'yer think they 'ad for breakfast?
Nice new chains an' a helping of the whiplash.

10. What d'yer think they had for dinner?
Belayin'-pin soup an' a squeeze thro' the wringer.

11. What d'yer think they had for supper?
    Oh, handspike hash an' a roll in the scuppers.

12. What d'yer think they had for carger?
    Black sheep that 'ave run the Embargo.

13. Blow today, an' blow termorrow,
    Blow for that ol' ship in sorrow.

ROLL THE COTTON DOWN

This favourite halyard shanty obviously was born in the cotton ports of the Southern States. Some versions sing of the port of Mobile only. One version in particular, being that used by the cotton screwers of these ports, has verses such as:

> We'll floor her off from fore to aft,
> There's five thousand bales for this 'ere craft.
>
> And bring yer sampson posts likewise,
> Bear a hand, git a curve on boys.
>
> Oh, tier by tier we'll stow 'em neat,
> Until the bloody job's complete.

tell much of the story behind the words "screwing cotton".

Our version is of a ship leaving San Francisco for Mobile Bay, and although given here as a halyard shanty, this was sometimes given a full chorus and made into a capstan song. The chorus ran:

> Roll the cotton!
> Roll the cotton, Moses!
> Roll the cotton,
> Oh, roll the cotton down!

This shanty was a great favourite with German seamen, in fact they had two versions of it in their own language, not to mention that they often sang it in English.

In the eighth verse, the shantyman is dropping a not-so-gentle hint to the officer of the watch to bring the ship closer to the wind, so as to luff her (shake the upper sails a little), in order to make the job of hauling the tops'l aloft a little easier.

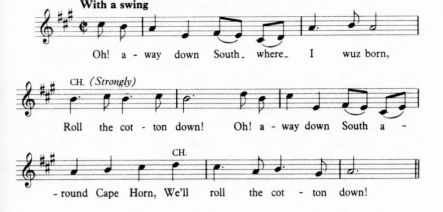

With a swing

Oh! a - way down South_ where_ I wuz born,

CH. *(Strongly)*

Roll the cot - ton down! Oh! a - way down South a -

CH.

- round Cape Horn, We'll roll the cot - ton down!

ROLL THE COTTON DOWN

1. Oh! away down South where I wuz born,
   Ch. Roll the cotton down!
   Oh! away down South around Cape Horn,
   Ch. We'll roll the cotton down!

2. Oh, away down south around Cape Horn,
   Oh, we wisht to Christ we'd niver bin born.

3. Oh, around Cape Stiff we are bound to go,
   Around Cape Stiff through the ice an' snow.

4. We're outward bound to Mobile Bay,
   We're outward bound at the break o' day.

5. Oh, Frisco town is far behind,
   Oh, the gals down south are free an' kind.

6. An' when we gits to Mobile town,
   All hands will roll the cotton down.

7. Oh, rock 'n' shake 'er is the cry,
   Oh, the bloody topm'st sheave is dry.

8. Oh, I wish Jackshite would keep his luff,
   The bastard thinks we've hauled enough.

9. Oh, stretch yer backs an' haul away,
   We'll make the port an' take our pay.

10. Oh, Mobile Bay's no place for me,
   I'll sail away to some other sea.

BLOOD-RED ROSES

This halyard shanty is a real "Cape Horner". It probably started life around the turn of the nineteenth century, perhaps even in the latter part of the eighteenth century. It appears to have been based on an older folk-song called *The Bunch o' Roses*, a song dealing with the Napoleonic wars. In fact, this expression "Blood-red Roses" is thought by some to be the name used by Napoleon's troops for the red-coated British soldiers of that period. The shanty may have started aboard troopships, and in the refrain one can almost hear the bosun shouting to the "leathernecks" : "Hang down, ye land-lubbers, heavy arses! Hang! ye bloody roses . . . !" and so on, as he roped them in to hoist the heavy tops'ls. Of course the sailormen would be engaged on more seamanlike work aloft. Soldiers had to work in the general running of these early troopships. The solos obviously apply to a later trade, that of the nitrate and guano carriers in which ships this shanty was popular.

Some versions have the refrain "Come down, ye bunch o' roses!" and others have "Go down, ye bunch o' roses!" but I prefer the "hanging" version. This expression was a common one under sail— "Hang down, me hearties!" was a daily sing-out when taking a pull at the braces or "sweating up" halyards, that is, giving them an extra pull to get them as tight as a bar. This shanty has the unusual form, be it noted, of four solos and four refrains in each verse.

YE BLOOD-RED ROSES

1. Me bonnie bunch o' roses O!
    Ch. Hang down, ye blood-red roses, hang down!
'Tis time for us to roll 'n' go!
    Ch. Hang down, ye blood-red roses, hang down!
Ooh! ye pinks 'n' posies,
    Ch. Hang down, ye blood-red roses, hang down!
Ooh! ye pinks 'n' posies,
    Ch. Hang down, ye blood-red roses, hang down!

2. We're bound out to Iquique Bay,
    We're bound away at the break of day.

3. We're bound away around Cape Horn,
    We wisht ter hell we'd niver bin born.

185

4. Around Cape Horn we all must go,
   Around Cape Stiff through the ice an' snow.

5. Me boots an' clothes are all in pawn,
   An' it's bleedin' draughty around Cape Horn.

6. 'Tis growl ye may but go ye must,
   If ye growl too hard yer head they'll bust.

8. The gals are waitin' right ahead,
   A long strong pull should shift the dead.

8. Them Spanish whores are pullin' strong,
   Hang down, me boys, it won't take long.

9. Oh, rock an' shake 'er is the cry,
   The bloody topm'st sheave is dry.

10. Just one more pull an' that'll do,
    We're the buckos fer ter kick 'er through.

JOHN KANAKA

This halyard song is the only known representative of a sizeable group of Anglicized Polynesian work-songs popular at one time among seamen in the various Pacific Islands trades. Dana, in his TWO YEARS BEFORE THE MAST, refers to such songs and the singing of them by Mahana, an Hawaiian shantyman in the hide carriers of the Pacific Slope of America in the 1830s.

The one we give here appears to have Samoan connections. However, it was not limited to ships in the Pacific Island trades, this one being very popular in most American sailing ships of the mid-nineteenth century. The writer collected this version from a coloured seaman from Barbados, in the West Indies. Apart from work-songs, we know from Mr Gale Huntington's excellent book SONGS THE WHALEMEN SANG that many other Anglicized Marquesan and Tahitian songs were top favourites with the South Sea sperm whalers. It is a great pity that so many of these interesting and curiously romantic songs have been allowed to pass into oblivion. *John Kanaka* is one of the few representatives of the three-line solo and three-line refrain shanties. The "oh" in the third solo, when sung by a good shantyman, was always rendered with a hitch (a sort of wild yelp).

With a swing

I heard, I heard the Old Man say, John Ka-
-na-ka-na-ka tulai - ē! To - day, to - day
is a ho - li - - day. John Ka-
-na-ka-na-ka tu - lai - ē! Tu - lai e - oh! tu - lai -
ē! John Ka - na - ka - na - ka tu - lai - ē!

JOHN KANAKA

1. I heard, I heard the Old Man say,
   Ch. John Kanaka-naka, tulai-e!
Today, today is a holiday,
   Ch. John Kanaka-naka, tulai-e!
Tulai-e, ooh! tulai-e!
   Ch. John Kanaka-naka, tulai-e!

2. We'll work termorrer, but no work terday,
We'll work termorrer, but no work terday,

3. We're bound away for Frisco Bay,
We're bound away at the break o' day.

4. We're bound away around Cape Horn,
We wish ter Christ we'd niver bin born.

5. A Yankee ship wid a Yankee crew,
Oh, we're the buckos fer ter push 'er through.

6. A Yankee ship wid a Yankee mate,
If yer stop ter walk he'll change yer gait.

7. Oh, haul away, oh, haul away!
Oh, haul away, an' make yer pay!

WHISKEY JOHNNY

This halyard shanty was one that had innumerable verses and versions. We have taken some of the best verses from each of the different versions and spliced them into ours—the sort of thing any good shantyman would do in a long hoist. The only version from which we have not borrowed anything is the obscene one based on the ancient *Crabfish Song*, a rather respectable version of which is given in Bishop Percy's RELIQUES. Many of the stanzas starting "If whiskey wuz a . . ." are to be found in Negro folk-song. Shanghai Brown, referred to in the eleventh verse, was a notorious crimp of the Barbary Coast, Frisco, who operated towards the latter end of the nineteenth century.

This shanty was a favourite at the mizen tops'l halyards, in a full-rigged ship, the reason being that the hands had to invade the holy poop in order to perform this chore, and the shantyman, always hopeful, imagined that his suggestive solos about a "dram" would open the Old Man's heart. If they did, a "splice the main brace" (issue of rum) would be the result. It is rather strange that a work-song singing of whiskey ever became so popular with seamen, seeing that it was rarely a seafarer's tipple, with the exception, perhaps, of the rotgut rye dished out by the crimps of the Barbary Coast, the outcome of drinking which invariably put the imbiber aboard of an outward-bound hell-ship.

Rather fast

Oh, whis - key is the life of man,

CH. Whis - key John - ny! Ooh! Whis - key from an

ol' tin can, Whis - key for me John - ny!

WHISKEY JOHNNY

1. Oh, whiskey is the life of man,
    Ch. Whiskey Johnny!
   Ooh! Whiskey from an ol' tin can,
    Ch. Whiskey for me Johnny!

2. Whiskey here, whiskey there!
   Oooh! whiskey almost everywhere.

3. Whiskey up an' whiskey down,
   Oooh! whiskey all around the town.

4. Whiskey made me pawn me clothes,
   Whiskey gave me this red nose.

5. Some likes whiskey, some likes beer,
   I wisht I had a barrel here.

6. If I can't have whiskey then I'll have rum,
   That's the stuff ter make good fun.

7. Oh, the mate likes whiskey an' the skipper likes rum,
   The sailors like both but we can't git none.

8. A tot of whiskey fer each man,
   An' a bloody big bottle fer the shantyman.

9. If whiskey wuz a river an' I could swim,
   I'd say 'ere goes an' dive right in.

10. If whiskey wuz a river an' I wuz a duck,
    I'd dive to the bottom an' I'd niver come up.

11. If yiz ever go to Frisco town,
    Mind ye steer clear o' Shanghai Brown.

12. He'll dope yer whiskey night an' morn,
    An' he'll then shanghai yiz round Cape Horn.

13. There wuz a Limejuice skipper o' the name o' Hogg,
    Once tried to stop his sailors' grog.

14. Which made the crew so weak an' slack,
    That the helmsman caught 'er flat aback.

15. An' ever after so they say,
    That crew got grog three times a day.

16. Whiskey made the Ol' Man say,
    Give one more pull, lads, then belay!

HANGING JOHNNY

This hauling song was usually started at to'gallant halyards, and was even used for sweatin'-up. One or two verses only would be used in this latter case. This was one pulling song that was sung slow or fast, depending on the shantyman and the job in hand.

It has been suggested that the Hanging Johnny of this sailor work-song was none other than the infamous Jack Ketch, hangman of the reign of Charles II. Another notorious hangman called Derrick, of the reign of Elizabeth I, is also supposed to have given his name to the shipboard crane commonly called a "derrick".

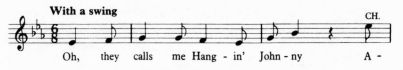

HANGING JOHNNY

1. Oh, they calls me Hangin' Johnny,
   Ch. Away, boys, away!
   They sez I hangs for money,
   Ch. So-o, hang, boys, hang!

2. They sez I hangs fer money,
   But hangin' is so funny.

3. At first I hanged me daddy,
   An' then I hanged me mammy.

4. Oh, yes, I hanged me mother,
   Me sister an' me brudder.

5. I hanged me sister Sally,
   I hanged the whole damned family.

6. An' then I hanged me granny,
   I hanged her up quite canny.

7. I'd hang all mates an' skippers,
   I'd hang 'em by their flippers.

8. I'd hang a bloody copper,
   I'd give him the long dropper.

9. I'd hang the bleedin' bosun,
   The dirty, rotten whoreson.

10. A rope, a beam, a ladder,
    I'd hang ye all tergether.

11. We'll hang an' haul tergether,
    We'll hang fer better weather.

12. We'll hang 'em to the yard-arm,
    Hang the sea an' buy a pig-farm.

193

BONEY

As well as being a halyard shanty, Boney was occasionally used as a sheet or short-haul song. Obviously it was born during or shortly after the Napoleonic Wars. Some think it was based on the French seamen's hauling song *Jean François de Nantes*, but I rather fancy the reverse occurred. In the hands of most shantymen its narrative was a fairly historical one, although some singers did have Boney crossing the Rockies. This was one shanty in which the common shore folk-song style of pronouncing all short "i" sounds as "eye" was rather overdone by some singers. The "Franswor" in the refrains is, of course, the French name "François". In the twelfth verse, the "Billy Ruffian" is the sailor pronunciation of the British man-o'-war Bellerophon which took Napoleon as a prisoner to St Helena. Boney is one of the very few shanties which, as far as I know, has no obscene version.

The fifth verse contains a rather deeply hidden sailor quip. A "Frenchman" or "Frenchyman" is the term given to an underhand turn put in a rope when coiling up a fall. German sailors call this method of coiling "putting in an Englander". In both cases the member of the race named is thought to be underhanded by the user.

BONEY

1. Boney was a war-rye-or,
   Ch. Way-aye-yah!
   A war-rye-or, a ter-rye-or,
   Ch. Johnny Franswor!

2. Boney beat the Prussians,
   The Osstrye-ans an' the Rooshye-ans,

3. Boney went to school in France,
   He learnt to make the Rooshians dance.

4. Oh, Boney marched to Moscow,
   Lost his army in the snow.

5. Boney wuz a Frenchyman,
   But Boney had to turn again.

6. He wuz sent to Elba,
   Wisht he'd niver bin there.

7. He whacked the Proosians squarely,
   He beat the English nearly.

8. We licked him Trafalgar's Bay,
   Carried his main topm'st away.

9. 'Twas on the Plains of Waterloo,
   He met the boy who put 'm through.

10. He met the Duke o' Wellington,
    An' then his downfall wuz begun.

11. The long-nosed Dook he put him through,
    He put 'im through at Waterloo.

12. Boney went a-cru-sye-in,
    Aboard the Billy Ruf-fye-an.

13. They sent him into exile,
    He died on St Helena's Isle.

14. Boney was a war-rye-or,
    He rorty, snorty war-rye-or.

HAUL THE BOWLINE

The whys-and-wherefores of this sheet shanty have been discussed at length in the main body of this work, leaving little to add here. The final word of the refrain, "Haul!" on which the pull came, was in some ships altered to "Pull!" although in most cases it was just a wild yell given as the men fell back and downwards in a vicious concerted drag. In its present form, this shanty was usually associated with the port of Liverpool, and Kitty of Liverpool was rarely, if ever, omitted by the shantyman. The "chafin' leather" in the eleventh verse was a long strip of pigskin, sewn over the boltrope of the leeches and foot of a squaresail at positions where chafe was liable to be caused by the shrouds when the sheet was hauled aft. Another method of preventing chafe in such circumstances was to have chafing-battens or "Scotchmen" covering the shrouds at positions where the boltrope of the sail would constantly rub.

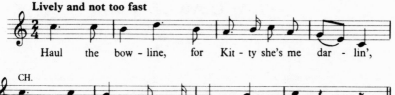

Lively and not too fast

Haul the bow - line, for Kit - ty she's me dar - lin',

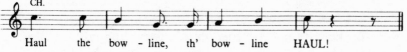

CH.

Haul the bow - line, th' bow - line HAUL!

HAUL THE BOWLINE

1. Haul the bowline—for Kitty she's me darlin',
   Ch. Haul the bowline, th' bowline HAUL!

2. Haul the bowline—Kitty lives in Liverpool.

3. Haul the bowline—Liverpool's a fine town.

4. Haul the bowline—so earlye in the mornin'.

5. Haul the bowline—before the day wuz dawnin'.

6. Haul the bowline—the Cape Horn gale's a-howlin'.

7. Haul the bowline—the cook he is a-growlin'.

8. Haul the bowline—we'll either break or bend it.

9. Haul the bowline—we're men enough ter mend it.

10. Haul the bowline—we'll haul away tergether.

11. Haul the bowline—an' burst the chafin' leather.

12. Haul the bowline—we'll hang for finer weather.

HAUL AWAY, JOE

This was another sheet shanty with the pull coming on the final word of the refrain, ". . . Joe" in this case; although, as in the previous shanty, this was often no more than a savage howl. This shanty was always sung in an Irish brogue as were some other sailor worksongs. The line in the fifth verse about the "plaster" is from a shore folk-song *Aunt Jemima's Plaster*, and the verse singing of the "King of France" was one never omitted, at least aboard British ships. Twelve verses are given here, although when hauling on the fore sheet no more than three or four at the most would be used. However, since there exist even more than twelve verses, the writer has a feeling that at some time or other this shanty must have been used at halyards, or at least at a long hoist of some sort. The gals of "Booble Alley" mentioned in the ninth verse, and the "round-the-corner Sallies", were two types of old-time prostitutes, the former being brothel girls, the latter street-walkers. Booble Alley was a notorious street in the old Liverpool sailor-town, and is mentioned by Melville in his book REDBURN. In the eleventh verse, "put square-head on him" means that he was bashed about.

Slow and deliberate

Hey, don't yer see___ that black cloud a - ris - in'?

CH.

'Way, haul a - way,___ we'll haul a - way Joe!

HAUL AWAY, JOE

1. Hey, don't yer see that black cloud a-ris-in'?
Ch. 'Way, haul away, we'll haul away, Joe!
Hey, don't yer see that black cloud a-ris-in'?
Ch. 'Way, haul away, we'll haul away Joe!

2. Naow whin Oi wuz a little boy, an' so me mother told me,
That if Oi didn't kiss the gals me lips would all grow mouldy.

3. Oi sailed the seas for many a year, not knowin' what Oi wuz
missin',
Then Oi sets me sails afore the gales an' started in a-kissin'.

4. Naow first Oi got me a Spanish gal an' she wuz fat an' lazy,
An' then Oi got a nigger tart—she nearly druv me crazy.

5. Oi found meself a Yankee gal—she wasn't very civil,
So Oi stuck a plaster on her back, an' sent 'er to the divil.

6. Then Oi got meself an' Oirish gal an' her name wuz Flannigan,
She stole me boots, she stole me clothes, she stole me plate
an' pannikin.

7. Oi courted then a Frenchy gal, she sure tooks things free an'
aisy,
But naow Oi've got me an English gal an' sure she is a daisy.

8. So list, me boys, while Oi sing ter ye about me darlin' Nancy,
She's coppered-bottom, clipper-built, she's jist me style an'
fancy.

9. Ye may talk about yer Yankee gals an' round-the-corner Sallies,
But they couldn't make the grade me boys wid the gals of
Booble Alley.

10. King Louis wuz the king o' France afore the revolu-shye-un,
But the people cut his head right orf an' spoiled his
consti-too-shye-un.

11. They sent the King away ter sea—to larn him 'ow ter swim,
Oh, they sent him wid a Bluenose mate who put square-head
on him.

12. Oh, once Oi wuz in Oireland a-diggin' turf an' taties,
But naow Oi'm on a Limejuice ship a-haulin' on the braces.

DONKEY RIDING

As stated in the text, as well as being a capstan shanty this was a favourite with stevedores, in particular those in the timber trade, and also among the Mobile Bay cotton hoosiers. It is a variant of *Hieland Laddie*, and related to *Because She Was a Young Thing Lately Left Her Mammy O*—a shore-song found in various parts of Britain—this, in its turn, having kinship with *Billy Boy* in both its sea and land versions. The Broomielaw, in the eighth verse, was the famous Sailortown of Glasgow in the days of the packet ships. The final line of each verse as sung by John Salt was usually of the veriest filth. Something not quite understood by shore folk-song singers is the fact that the sailor rarely used *double entendre*, such as the sexual symbolism of "fiddles", "knapsacks" and so on, examined by James Reeves in his IDIOM OF THE PEOPLE. No sir! Sailor John called a spade a spade, and all his dirty lines were filthy in the extreme. Later, we give one of the very few songs in which the sailor did make use of a nautical *double entendre*—the *Ratcliffe Highway*.

Lively

Wuz ye ev - er in Que-bec, laun-chin' tim-ber on the deck, Where ye'd break yer bleed-in' neck

CH.

Rid-in' on a don-key?' Way, hay, an' a-way we go!

FULL CH

Don-key rid-ing, don-key rid-in'! Way, hay an' a-way we go! Oh, rid-in' on a don-key!

DONKEY RIDING

1. Wuz ye ever in Quebec,
Launchin' timber on the deck,
Where ye'd break yer bleedin' neck,
   Ch. Ridin' on a donkey?

   Full chorus. Way, hay, an' away we go!
            Donkey riding, donkey riding!
            Way, hay, an' away we go!
            Riding on a donkey!

2. Wuz ye ever in Timbuktoo,
Where the gals are black an' blue,
Where they waggle their backsides too,
   Ch. Riding on a donkey?

3. Wuz ye ever in Vallipo,
Where them gals put on a show,
Waggle an' wriggle wid a roll 'n' go,
   Ch. Riding on a donkey?

202

4. Wuz ye ever down Mobile Bay,
   Screwin' cotton all the day,
   A dollar a day is a White Man's pay,
   Ch. Riding on a donkey?

5. Wuz ye ever in Canton,
   Where the men wear pigtails long,
   An' the gals play hong-ki-kong,
   Ch. Riding on a donkey?

6. Wuz ye ever in London town,
   Where them gals they do come down,
   To see the king in a golden crown,
   Ch. Riding on a donkey?

7. Wuz ye ever in Mirramashee,
   Where ye tie up to a tree,
   An' the skeeters do bite we,

8. Wuz ye ever on the Broomielaw,
   Where them Yanks is all the go,
   An' the gals dance heel an' toe,
   Ch. Riding on a donkey?

9. Wuz ye ever down Frisco Bay,
   Where the gals all shout hooray,
   Here comes Johnny wid his three years pay,
   Ch. Riding on a donkey?

10. Wuz ye ever off Cape Horn,
    Where yer backside's never warm,
    When yiz wish ter hell ye'd niver bin born,
    Ch. Riding on a donkey?

This stamp 'n' go song or "runaway chorus" as sailors often called this type of shanty is fairly certain to be of Negro origin. Its theme on shore was a religious one, in which the gambler, harlot, sinner and drunkard all "got in the way", and the "chariot bound to heav'n" would stop and pick up the unfortunate rake. When the devil got in the way, however, the golden chariot would "run over" him. These early shore versions were reported to be found all over Negro America by early collectors. In later days, the Salvation Army and other revivalists sang versions, and it has even turned up as a "pep song" at baseball games. The old-time sailor, judging from his songs, appears to agree with Doctor Johnson in his preference for a night in gaol rather than aboard ship.

Boisterously

Oh, a drop of Nel-son's blood wouldn't do us an-y harm, Oh, a drop of Nel-son's blood would-n't do us an-y harm, Oh, a drop of Nel-son's blood would-n't do us an-y harm, An' we'll all hang on be-hind! So we'll ro-o-oll the ol' cha-ri-ot a-long! An' we'll roll the gold-en cha-riot a-long! Oh, we'll ro-o-oll the ol' cha-ri-ot a-long, An' we'll all hang on be-hind!

ROLL THE OLD CHARIOT

1. Oh, a drop of Nelson's blood wouldn't do us any harm,
Oh, a drop of Nelson's blood wouldn't do us any harm,
Oh, a drop of Nelson's blood wouldn't do us any harm,
Ch. And we'll all hang on behind!

Full Chorus. So we'll ro-o-oll the old chariot along!
An' we'll roll the golden chariot along!
Oh, we'll ro-o-oll the old chariot along!
An' we'll all hang on behind!

2. Oh, a plate of Irish stew wouldn't do us any harm. (*Three times*)

3. Oh, a nice fat cook wouldn't do us any harm.

4. Oh, a roll in the clover wouldn't do us any harm.

5. Oh, a long spell in gaol wouldn't do us any harm.

6. Oh, a nice watch below wouldn't do us any harm.

7. Oh, a night with the gals wouldn't do us any harm.

8. Oh, a job on a farm wouldn't do us any harm.

PADDY DOYLE'S BOOTS

This was the only shanty dedicated to the bunting of a sail, although one or two other sailor writers declare that *Johnny Boker*, a short drag or sheet shanty, was also at times used for this chore. Paddy Doyle is said to have been a boarding-house master of Liverpool somewhere around the mid and late nineteenth century. He was also a ship tailor and, like many of their ilk, a proper sailor-robber. However, it would appear one sailor got to wind'ard of him by bilking him of a pair of sea-boots. Whether Paddy Doyle actually lived or was merely a figure of sailor legend it is difficult to say, since evidence of his existence is meagre. Sometimes tales relating to him are not his at all but belong to Paddy West, whose song follows next.

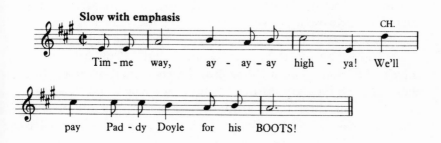

PADDY DOYLE'S BOOTS

1. Timme way, ay-ay-ay high-ya!
We'll pay Paddy Doyle for his BOOTS!

2. Timme way-ay-ay-ay high ya!
We'll all throw muck at the cook!

3. Timme way-ay-ay-ay high ya!
We'll all shave under the chin!

4. Timme way-ay-ay-ay high ya!
We'll all drink whiskey an' gin!

PADDY WEST

This famous forebitter is built around the exploits of a nefarious Liverpool boarding-house keeper called Paddy West. He lived, so old-timers say, in Dennison Street, or Great Howard Street, Liverpool, although one old seaman seems to think he had his boarding-house off London Road. Anyhow the main difference between Paddy and other boarding-house masters and crimps was the fact that he "schooled" his potential ships' crews in a singular fashion.

Anyone wishing to join a ship had to stay at Paddy's domicile for a week, no more. During this week, tinker, tailor, counter-jumper or dish-washer would be given sufficient "larnin" to turn him into an Able Seaman—the normal period of such a transformation taking four years. Paddy would get the candidate to stand in the backyard where he had a ship's wheel rigged up, and put him through the mysteries of steering. During this operation Paddy's wife would throw a bucket of water over the "cadet" to get him used to the "cold nor'westers". Then the aspiring pupil would be chased up to the attic to furl the "windy-blind"—"practice in stowing canvas", Paddy would state. But the final ritual of all was when the candidate had to step over a piece of string in the "passage", and then walk three times around the front-room table on which was placed a cow's horn. "Whin the mate axs ye what ships ye have sailed in, tell him, ye've crossed the Line and rounded the Horn— but don't tell him it was a bloody cow horn!" was the admonition the pupil would get from Paddy. Such ignorant sailors were usually demoted as soon as they got to sea, but the term "Paddy Wester" for a useless sailor is still sometimes to be heard around the water-front of Liverpool.

With a swing

Oh, as I wuz a - rol - lin' down Great How - ard

Street, I strolled in - to Pad - dy West's house. He—

gave me a plate of A - mer - i - can hash, an'

swore it wuz Eng - lish scouse, Sez he, 'Look 'ere— young

fel - ler, yer ve - ry jist in time, To— go a - way

in a big clip - per— ship, an' ve - ry soon ye'll sign.

CH.

Then its put on yer dun - ga - ree jac - ket

an' give the boys a rest, An'— think o' the cold— nor'

wes - ters that blow, In the house o' Pad - dy West's.

PADDY WEST

1. Oh, as I wuz a-rollin' down Great Howard Street,
   I strolled into Paddy West's house.
   He gave me a plate of American hash,
   An' swore it wuz English scouse,
   Sez he, "Look 'ere young feller, yer very just in time,
   To go away in a big clipper ship, an' very soon ye'll sign."

   Ch. Then it's put on yer dungaree jacket,
      An' give the boys a rest,
      An' think of the cold nor'westers that blow,
      In the house of Paddy West's!

2. Now he axed me if I had ever bin to sea,
   I told him not till that morn;
   "Well, be Jasus," sez he, "a sailor ye'll be,
   From the hour that yiz wuz born;
   Just go into the parlour, walk round the ol' cow horn,
   An' tell the mate that ye have bin, oh, three times round the
                                                      Horn!"

3. When I got into ol' Paddy West's house,
   The wind began to blow;
   He sent me up to the lumber-room,
   The fore-royal for to stow;
   When I climbed up to the attic, no fore-royal could I find,
   So I jumped upon the winder-sill and furled the winder-blind.

4. It's Paddy, me bhoy, he pipes all hands on deck,
   Their stations for to man.
   His wife, Sarry Ann, stood in the backyard,
   A bucket in her hand;
   His wife let go of the bucket, the water flew on its way;
   "Clew up yer fore t'gallant, me sons, she's takin' in a say!"

5. To every two men what graduates,
   I'll give wan outfit free,
   For two good men on watch at once
   Ye never need to see;
   Oilskins, me bhoys, ye won't want, carpet slippers made o' felt
   I will dish out to the pair o' ye, wid a ropeyarn for a belt.

RATCLIFFE HIGHWAY

The central theme of this song, that of a sailor getting mixed up with a Highway Harlot, is to be found in many songs called by the same name. However, the tunes of all of them are different and the theme usually branches into one of two endings—either the sailor gets robbed by or else he receives a "dose" of venereal disease from the Highway Harlot. In one version he gets robbed, but settles the issue in his favour by stealing a gold watch or something else of value from the prostitute. Another feature of such songs is that they are all couched in nautical *double entendre*—shipboard terms and orders partially disguising the sexual words and phrases implied. Although other examples of the cunning use of nautical terms do exist in sailor song, most of these are non-sexual. The *Sailor's Farewell* is one of the best-known songs using this other kind of camouflage. The only other sailor song the writer can call to mind in which the sexual imagery is of a nautical kind is the halyard shanty *Blow the Man Down*, which in one version makes use of Ratcliffe Highway themes. Our version here is one in which the sailor gets damaged "on a voyage to Cytherea" as Bone puts it. This forebitter is of great age and was popular at fo'c'sle sing-songs right to the end of Sail.

The famous Ratcliffe Highway, close to the London Docks, has had its name altered several times down through the years—at one time it was called Great George's Street—but on a recent visit to the neighbourhood I noticed that this once famous and notorious waterfront street now bears the name of The Highway. In the present writer's book SAILORTOWN, a complete description is given of The Highway—its pubs, its brothels, music-halls and fascinating characters of the days of sail.

As I wuz a-rol-lin' down the High-way one
morn, I spied a flash pac-ket from ol' Wap-ping
town, As soon as I seed her I slacked me main
brace, An' I hoist-ed me stun-s'ls an' to her gave
CH.
chase, Oh, me rig - gin's slack, Aye, me ratt - lin's are
frayed, I've ratt-led me rig-ging down Rat-cliffe High-way!

RATCLIFFE HIGHWAY

1. As I wuz a-rollin' down the Highway one morn,
   I spied a flash packet from ol' Wapping town,
   As soon as I seed her I slacked me main brace,
   An' I hoisted me stuns'ls an' to her gave chase.

   Ch. Oh, me riggin's slack,
   Aye, me rattlin's are frayed,
   I've rattled me rigging down Ratcliffe Highway!

2. Her flag wuz three colours, her masthead wuz low,
   She wuz round at the counter an' bluff at the bow;
   From larboard to starboard an' so rolled she,
   She wuz sailin' at large, she wuz runnin' free.

3. I fired me bow-chaser, the signal she knew,
   She backed her main tops'l an' for me hove to;
   I lowered down me jolly-boat an' rowed alongside,
   An' I found madam's gangway wuz open an' wide.

4. I hailed her in English, she answered me clear,
   "I'm from the Black Arrow bound to the Shakespeare";
   So I wore ship wid a what d'yer know,
   An' I passed her me hawser an' took her in tow.

5. I tipped her me flipper, me towrope an' all,
   She then let her hand on me reef-tackle fall;
   She then took me up to her lily-white room,
   An' in her main riggin' I fouled me jibboom.

6. I entered her little cubby-hole, an' swore damn yer eyes,
   She wuz nothin' but a fireship rigged up in disguise,
   She had a foul bottom, from sternpost to fore,
   'Tween wind and water she ran me ashore.

7. She set fire to me riggin', as well as me hull,
   An' away to the lazareet I had to scull;
   Wid me helm hard-a-starboard as I rolled along,
   Me shipmates cried, "Hey, Jack, yer mainyard is sprung!"

8. Now I'm safe in harbour, me moorings all fast,
   I lay here quite snug, boys, till all danger is past;
   With me mainyard all served, boys, an' parcelled an' tarred,
   Wasn't that a stiff breeze, boys, that sprung me mainyard?

9. Here's a health to the gal wid the black, curly locks,
   Here's a health to the gal who ran me on the rocks;
   Here's a health to the quack, boys, who eased me from pain,
   If I meet that flash packet I'll board her again.

THE GALS AROUND CAPE HORN

This forebitter was one which was popular with naval and merchant seamen alike. Like most forebitters it had several tunes, and the name of the ship concerned was different in each singer's mouth. It was equally popular with American as well as British seamen, although its land of origin is most certainly England. The earliest versions are naval, I would say, the merchantman's versions being of a much later date.

The fact that the ship concerned heads around the Horn and visits the ports of Chile suggests to the average listener that it is a song of the Merchant Service rather than of the Navy, but in fact prior to World War I a section of the British fleet was stationed out in this part of the world. It was known as the Pacific Squadron, with its headquarters at Esquimault in Canada, and it was the last squadron of the British Navy in which sailing ships—as opposed to the "Down funnel, up screw, make sail" type of ironclads—were to be found right to the end. With their single tops'ls with three rows of reefs and stuns'ls alow and aloft they made a brave sight when sailing in company.

Strong

Oh, 'tis of the pac - ket Am - phi - trite, In
Bris - tol she did lay, A - wait - in' there for
or - ders, boys, for to take us far a - way, A -
-wait - in' there for or - ders, boys, for to
take us far from home, An' our or - ders came for
Ri - o, boys, An' then a - round Cape Horn.____

THE GALS AROUND CAPE HORN

1. Oh, 'tis of the packet Amphitrite, in Boston she did lay,
Awaitin' there for orders, boys, for to take us far away,
Awaitin' there for orders, boys, for to take us far from home,
An' our orders came for Rio, boys, an' then around Cape
                                                          Horn.

2. Oh, we beat our way across the Bay, with a fair wind to the
                                                          Line,
The royals all set and the stays all taut, the Trades they blew
                                                          so fine;
Our Johns they all were fighting fit, good seamen all were we,
For to hand and reef and steer, me boys, we all worked
                                                          bravely.

3. When we arrived in Rio, boys, we anchored there a while,
   We set up all our rigging, and we bent all our new sail;
   From ship to ship they cheered us, as we did pass along,
   And they wished us pleasant weather in a-roundin' o' the
                                                         Horn.

4. When beatin' off Magellan Straits, the wind blew strong an'
                                                          hard,
   While short'ning sail two gallant tars fell from the tops'l yard;
   By angry seas the lines we threw from their weak hands was
                                                          torn,
   We had to leave 'em to the sharks that prowl around Cape
                                                         Horn.

5. When we got round the Horn, me lads, fine nights and
                                                 pleasant days,
   And the very next place we anchored in was Valparaiso Bay;
   Where all them pretty gals come down, I solemnly do swear,
   Oh, they're far above them Liverpool gals, with their dark
                                                and wavy hair.

6. They like a jolly sailorman when he is on the spree,
   They'll dance with you and drink with you and spend yer
                                                 money free;
   And when yer money is all gone, they'll not on you impose,
   Oh, they're far above them Yankee gals who'll steal an' pawn
                                                 yer clothes.

7. Farewell to Valparaiso, boys, along the Chile main,
   And likewise all them Spanish gals, they treated me just fine;
   An' if I live to get paid off I'll sit and drink all morn,
   A health to them dashing Spanish gals that live around Cape
                                                         Horn!

THE STATELY SOUTHERNER

This forebitter, although well known in the fo'c'sles of British sailing ships, is obviously of American origin. As stated earlier, it may have been composed about 1777 or 1778, shortly after John Paul Jones sailed up the Irish Sea in his privateer the *Ranger*, fired on coastal towns and worried British shipping. Although called *The Stately Southerner*, the *Ranger* was in no wise connected with the Southern States, being fitted out in Portsmouth, New Hampshire, and being manned by Northerners.

THE STATELY SOUTHERNER

1. Oh, it was a stately Southerner, as flew the stars and bars,
   An' the whistlin' wind from the west-n'-west rang thro' her
                                    pitch-pine spars,
   And with her tacks about, me boys, she hung upon the gale,
   'Twas an autumn night, when she made the light, of the ol'
                                    Head of Kinsale.

2. It was a fine an' cloudless night, the wind blew fresh an'
                                    strong,
   As gaily 'cross the Channel wave our good ship bowl'd along;
   An' the foam beneath her tramplin' bows the rollin' waves
                                    did spread,
   An, as she stooped low, with her breast o' snow, she buried
                                    her lee cathead.

_3._ There was no talk of short'ning sail by him who trod the
poop,
And under the weight of the ponderous jib her boom bent
like a hoop;
An' the groanin' chesstrees told the strain held down by the
stout main tack,
But he only laughed as he gazed abaft at her bright an'
glitterin' track.

_4._ The mid-tide met in the Channel waves that flow from shore
to shore,
The mist lay thick along the land from Featherstone to
Dunmore;
Yet gleamed the light on Tuskar Rock where the bell still
tolled the hour,
But the beacon light that shone so bright was quenched on
Waterford Tower.

_5._ The canvas that our good ship bore was tops'ls fore an' aft,
Her spanker too and standing jib for she was a stiffish craft;
"All hands aloft!" our Old Man cried. "Loose out yer light
sail fast!"
And t'gans'ls all an' royals small soon swelled upon each mast.

_6._ What looms upon our starboard bow, what hangs upon the
breeze?
'Tis time the packet hauled her wind abreast the old Saltees;
For by the mighty press of sail that clothed each lofty spar,
That ship we spied on the misty tide was a British man-o'-war.

_7._ "Out booms, out booms!" our skipper cried. "Out booms
an' give her sheet!"
And the swiftest keel that ever was launched shot ahead of the
British fleet;
And amidst a thund'ring shower o' shot, with stuns'ls hoistin'
away,
Down Channel clear, Paul Jones did steer, just at the break o'
day.

RUDE BOREAS

Since we have given this curious song full treatment on page 21, there is little left to say here. Boreas, of course, was the Classical god of the north wind, usually depicted high up in the northern latitudes on ancient charts as a bearded deity, figurehead only, with a whole gale coming from his pursed lips. He is often mentioned in the ballad-makers' broadsheets on the eighteenth and nineteenth centuries. Although possibly of shore origin, this song was accepted by seamen and stood the test of time, since it was being sung aboard men-o'-war even in my father's time. It was usually sung with many "twiddles and quavers", and in the middle passages a certain amount of syncopation was employed. This jazz effect was often used by the old-time seamen when singing their leisure songs—in fact long before the days when jazz became popular.

Come rude Bo - reas,____ blust -'ring rai -ler,____

List ye lands - men all__ to me,____ Ship- mates

hear_ a bro - ther sai - lor____ sing of the

dan - gers of__ the sea.____ From bound- ing bil - lows,

first in mo - tion, When the dis - tant whirl -winds

rise,____ To the tem - pest trou-bled o - cean,

____ When the skies__ con-tend with skies.____

RUDE BOREAS

1. Come rude Boreas, blustering railer, list ye landsmen all to me,
Shipmates hear a brother sailor sing of the dangers of the sea.
From bounding billows, first in motion, when the distant
whirlwinds rise,
To the tempest-troubled ocean, when the skies contend with
skies.

2. Hark the bosun's hoarsely bawlin', by tops'l sheets an'
halyards stand,
   Down t'gans'ls quick be haulin', down yer stays'ls, hard, boys,
hard!
   See it freshens, set taut the braces, tops'ls sheets now let go,
   Luff, boys, luff, don't make wry faces, up yer tops'ls nimbly
clew.

3. Now all ye on downbeds a-sportin', fondly locked in Beauty's
arms,
   Fresh enjoyments, wanton courtin', safe from all but love
alarms;
   Round us roars the angry tempest, see what fears our minds
enthrall,
   Harder yet, it blows still harder, hark again the bosun's call.

4. The tops'l yard points to the wind bows, see all clear to reef
each course,
   Let the foresheet go, don't mind, boys, tho' the weather
should be worse;
   Fore 'n' aft the sprits'l yard get, reef the mizen, see all clear,
   Hands up each preventer-brace get, man the fore-yard, cheer,
boys, cheer!

5. All the while fierce thunder's roarin', peel on peel contendin'
flash,
   On our heads fierce rain falls pourin', in our eyes blue
lightnings flash;
   All around us one wide water, all above us one black sky,
   Different deaths at once surround us, hark! what means that
dreadful cry?

6. The foremast's gone! cries every tongue out, o'er the lee
twelve foot above deck,
   A leak there is beneath the chesstrees sprung, pipe all hands
to clear the wreck;
   Come cut the lanyards all to pieces, come, me hearts, be stout
an' bold,
   Plumb the well, the leak increases, four foot water in the hold.

7. O'er the ship the wild waves beatin', we for wives and
children moan,
   Alas from here there's no retreatin', alas, to them there's no
return;
   Still the leak is gainin' on us, both chain-pumps are jammed
below,
   Heaven have mercy here upon us, for only that can save us
now.

8. On the lee beam there is land, boys, let the guns overboard
                                                be thrown,
   To the pump come every hand, boys, see our mizen mast is
                                                gone;
   The leak we've found it can't pour faster, we've lightened her
                                                a foot or more,
   Up an' rig a jury foremast, she's right, she's right, boys, we're
                                                off shore.

9. Now once more on shore we're thinkin', since kind Heaven
                                                has saved our lives,
   Come the cup now let's be drinkin' to our sweethearts an' our
                                                wives;
   Fill it up, about ship wheel it, close to our lips a-brimmin'
                                                fine,
   Where's the tempest, now, who feels it? None! the danger's
                                                drowned in wine!

THE FLYING CLOUD

This forebitter was a prime favourite with both British and American seamen, although more than likely its origin was Ireland. Illicit slaving and piracy are both covered in the song, thus putting its date somewhere around the early part of the nineteenth century, say 1825, shortly after the period when America and some European naval powers between them were supposed to have put an end to these evils—at least, on paper. It is a known fact, however, that illicit slaving and piracy were both in being for thirty years or more after such punitive exercises were believed to have cleaned up the waters of the West Indies and West Africa.

The ship in the song has never been identified, nor has its captain. Probably both are fictitious. Fifteen verses or more are known, some giving a vivid picture of the awful "Middle Passage" between Africa and America. Doerflinger, in his *Shantymen and Shantyboys*, believes that the composer of this song probably based his text on the confession of one of the crew of the notorious pirate Benito de Soto. This confession is to be found in a curious little paper-covered twelve-and-a-half cent book called the DYING DECLARATION OF NICHOLAS FERNANDEZ. There is certainly a great resemblance between the song and the confession.

My name is Ed - ward Hol - lan - der as

you may un - der - stand, I was born in the Ci - ty of

Wa - ter - ford in E - rin's love - ly land— When

I was young an' in me prime an' beau - ty on me

shone— Me pa - rents do - ted on___ me, 'Cos

I was___ their on - ly son.

THE FLYING CLOUD

1. My name is Edward Hollander as you may understand,
   I was born in the City of Waterford in Erin's lovely land.
   When I was young an' in me prime an' beauty on me shone,
   Me parents doted on me, 'cos I was their only son.

2. My father he rose up one morn an' wid him I did go,
   He bound me as a butcher boy to Kearney's of Wicklow;
   I wore the bloody apron there for three long years or more,
   Then I shipped aboard the *Erin's Queen* the pride of ol'
                                             Tramore.

3. 'Twas when we reached Bermuda's Isle I met wid Capen
                                                        Moore,
   The master of the *Flying Cloud*, the pride of Baltimore;
   An' I undertook to sail wid him, on a slavin' voyage to go,
   To the burnin' shores o' Africay, where the sugar-cane do
                                                        grow.

4. Oh, all went well until we came to Africay's sunny shore,
   Five hundred of them slaves, me boys, from their native land
                                                        we bore;
   Oh, each man loaded down wid chains as we made 'em march
                                                        below,
   Just eighteen inches space, me boy, oh, each man had to show.

5. The plague it came an' fever, too, an' took 'em off like flies,
   We had the niggers up on deck an' hove 'em in the tide;
   'Twas better for the rest o' them if they had died before,
   Than to drag the chain and feel the lash in Cuba for evermore.

6. An' now our money is all gone we must go to sea for more,
   So each man stayed an' listen'd to the words o' Capen Moore;
   "There's gold an' silver to be had, if with me you remain,
   Let's hoist the pirate flag aloft an' sweep the Spanish Main!"

7. We sank an' plundered many a ship down on the Spanish
                                                        Main,
   Left many a wife an' orphan child in sorrow to remain;
   To them we gave no quarter but we gave them watery graves,
   For a sayin' of our Capen was that dead men tell no tales.

8. Pursued were we by many a ship, by frigates and liners, too,
   Until a British man-o'-war, the *Dungemore*, hove in view;
   A shot then killed our Capen Moore an' twenty of our men,
   An' a bomb-shell set our ship on fire, we had to surrender
                                                        then.

9. An' now to Newgate we must go bound down wid iron chains,
   For the sinkin' an' the plunderin' of ships on the Spanish
                                                        Main;
   The judge he found us guilty, an' we are condemned to die,
   Young man a warnin' by me take an' shun all piracy!

THE BANKS OF NEWFOUNDLAND

The earliest form of this forebitter was a transportation ballad called *Van Dieman's Land*:

Ye ramblin' boys of Liverpool, I'll have ye to beware,
'Tis when ye go a-huntin' wid yer dog, yer gun, yer snare;
Watch out, boys, for the gamekeepers, keep yer dog at yer
command,
Just think on all them hardships goin' to Van Dieman's Land.

In the days of the old convict ships it was often heard sung ashore in Liverpool and also, in that form, was sung by seamen as a forebitter. By the 1820s, a change had taken place in the ballad. The Western Ocean packet rats took a hand in the matter and composed stanzas more suitable to their trade. This is the song we present here. The tune is obviously Irish and the text was sung in imitative Irish fashion. "Marrybone" mentioned in the song, also sometimes pronounced "Marrowbone", is a part of Liverpool called Marybone. This forebitter was usually sung with many "twiddles and quavers" and through the nose, as were many of these old songs in days gone by. An alternative way of singing the chorus was:

For it's while we're here, we can't be there,
On the Banks o' Newf'n'land!

Rather slow

Ye ram - blin' boys o' Liv - er - pool, Ye sai - lor - men be - ware, When yiz go in a Yan - kee pac - ket ship, no__ dun - ga - ree jum - pers wear, But__ have a mon - key jac - ket all__ un - to yer com - mand, For there blows some cold__ nor' wes - ters on the Banks of__ New - f'n' - land, We'll wash 'er, an' we'll scrub 'er down wid ho - ly - stone an'__ sand, An' we'll bid a - dieu to the Vir - gin Rocks an' the Banks of__ New - f'n' - land.

CH.

THE BANKS OF NEWFOUNDLAND

1. Ye ramblin' boys o' Liverpool, ye sailormen beware,
When yiz go in a Yankee packet ship, no dungaree jumpers
wear;
But have a monkey jacket all unto yer command,
For there blows some cold nor'westers on the Banks of
Newf'n'land.

Ch. We'll wash 'er an' we'll scrub 'er down, wid holystone an'
sand,
An' we'll bid adieu to the Virgin Rocks an' the Banks o'
Newf'n'land.

2. We had one Lynch from Ballynahinch, Spud Murphy and
Moike Moore,
'Twas in the winter of seventy-three them sea-boys suffered
sore;
They popped their clothes in Liverpool, some sold them all
out o' hand,
Not thinkin' of them cold nor' winds on the Banks o'
Newf'n'land.

3. We had a lady passenger—Bridget Reilly wuz her name,
To her I promised marriage—on me she had a claim;
She tore up her red flannel drawers, me bhoys, to make
mittens for our hands,
For she could not see them sea-boys freeze, on the Banks o'
Newf'n'land.

4. I dreamt a dream the other night, an' t'ought I wuz at home,
I dreamt that me and my judee wuz back in Marry-bone;
We both wuz in the ale-house, wid a jug o' ale in hand,
Then I awoke an' found no joke, on the Banks o' Newf'n'land.

5. The mate comes up on the fo'c'slehead, an' loudly he does
roar,
Rattle 'er in, me lively lads, we're off Americay's shore;
Scrub the mud off of the deadman's face an' haul or ye'll be
damned,
For there blows some cold nor'westers on the Banks o'
Newf'n'land.

6. An' now we're off of the Hook, me bhoys, an' the land's all
hid wid snow,
Soon we'll see the pay-table, an' spend all night below;
Down to the docks they come in flocks, them pretty young
gals do stand,
Sayin' "It's snugger wid me than it is at sea, on the Banks o'
Newf'n'land!"

THE SAILOR'S WAY

This is a lively forebitter common in the fo'c'sles of British ships, and apparently, according to Bill Adams, at one time heard aboard American vessels. It has several tunes, the one we give here being the most modern. This, like most forebitters, is of Irish origin, the Irish Gaelic word "acushla" in the chorus meaning "sweetheart". Sometimes different terms for "sweetheart" would be sung in place of "acushla", words like "mavourneen", "little Sing Loo", "sweet little Marie" and so on. As well as being a forebitter it was also sung at the capstan or at the Downton pump in some ships. This song, too, was associated with the port of Liverpool.

THE SAILOR'S WAY

1. We've courted gay Peruvian gals, French gals an' Chinee,
Spanish gals an' Dutch gals too, an' dainty Japanee;
To far Australia, Honolulu, where th' Hawaiian maidens play,
Just a different gal in every port,
   Ch. An' that's the Sailor's Way.

Full Chorus. Then it's goodbye, acushla, we're off to sea again,
          Sailor Jack, always comes back, to the gal he's left
                             behind!

2. In calm or storm, in rain or shine, the shellback doesn't mind,
   When on the ocean swell, he'll work like hell, for the gal he's
   left behind;
   He beats it north, he runs far south, he doesn't get much pay,
   He's always on a losin' game,
   Ch. An' that's the Sailor's Way!

3. Oh, shinin' is the North Star, as it hangs on our stabbud bow,
   We're homeward bound for Liverpool town, an' our hearts
   are in it now;
   We've crossed the Line an' the Gulf Stream, bin round by
   Table Bay,
   We've rounded Cape Horn, we're home again,
   Ch. An' that's the Sailor's Way!

4. We'll get paid off in Liverpool, an' blow our money free,
   We'll eat an' drink an' have our fun, an' forget the ruddy sea;
   Oh, Johnny'll go to his sweet Marie, an' Pat wid his 'cushla
   play,
   But I'll git drunk, turn into me bunk,
   Ch. An' that's the Sailor's Way!

BIBLIOGRAPHY

Ashton, John, REAL SAILOR SONGS (Leadenhall Press, London, 1891).

Baltzer, R., KNURRHAHN, German and English Sea Songs and Shanties, 2 vols. (Verlag A. C. Ehlers, Kiel, 1936).

Beckett, Mrs Clifford, SHANTIES AND FOREBITTERS (J. Curwen & Sons Ltd, London, 1914).

Bone, Capt. David W., CAPSTAN BARS (Porpoise Press, Edinburgh, 1931).

Bradford, J. and A. Fagge, OLD SEA CHANTIES (Metzler & Co. Ltd, London, 1904).

Broadwood, Lucy E., "Early Chanty Singing and Ship Music", JOURNAL OF THE FOLK SONG SOCIETY (London, pp. 55–8, Vol. VIII).

Brochmann, H., OPSANG FRA SEILSKIBSTIDEN (Norske Förlags Kompani Ltd, Christiania, 1916).

Bullen, Frank T., and W. F. Arnold, SONGS OF SEA LABOUR (Swan & Co. Ltd, London, 1914).

Clark, G. E., SEVEN YEARS OF A SAILOR'S LIFE (Adams & Co., Boston, 1867). One of the first writers to use the word "chanty".

Clements, Rex, MANAVILINS (Heath Cranton Ltd, London, 1928). Sea-songs and Forebitters.

Colcord, Joanna C., ROLL AND GO (Heath Cranton Ltd, London, 1924).

Colcord, Joanna C., SONGS OF AMERICAN SAILORMEN, enlarged edition of ROLL AND GO (W. W. Norton & Co., New York, 1938).

Colcord, Joanna C., SONGS OF AMERICAN SAILORMEN, paperback reprint of the foregoing (Oak Publications, New York, 1964).

Creighton, Helen, SONGS AND BALLADS FROM NOVA SCOTIA (Toronto, 1932).

Dana, R. H., Jnr, TWO YEARS BEFORE THE MAST (Harper & Brothers, New York, 1840, many reprints since).

Davis, J., and Ferris Tozer, SAILOR SONGS OR "CHANTIES" (Boosey & Co. Ltd, London, 1887).

Dibdin, Charles, SEA SONGS, with a memoir by Thomas Dibdin (London, 1841).

Dibdin, Charles, SEA SONGS AND BALLADS BY DIBDIN AND OTHERS (Bell & Daldy, London, 1863).

Doerflinger, William Main, SHANTYMEN AND SHANTYBOYS (Macmillan Company, New York, 1951).

Durger, R. A., and R. E. Lingefelter, SONGS OF THE GOLDRUSH (Cambridge University Press, England).

Eckstorm, Fanny H., and Mary W. Smith, THE MINSTRELSY OF MAINE, (Boston, 1927).

Firth, C. H., NAVAL SONGS AND BALLADS (Naval Records Society, 1907).

Greenleaf, Elizabeth B., and Grace Y. Mansfield, SONGS OF NEWFOUNDLAND (Harvard University Press, Cambridge, Mass., 1933).

Hales, J. W., and Dr P. J. Furnivall (Eds.), BISHOP PERCY'S FOLIO MANUSCRIPT, 3 vols. (London, 1868).

Halliwell, J. O. (Ed.), THE EARLY NAVAL BALLADS OF ENGLAND (Percy Society, Library of Trinity College, Cambridge, 1841).

Harlow, F. P., THE MAKING OF A SAILOR (Marine Research Society, Salem, Mass., 1928).

Harlow, F., CHANTEYING ABOARD AMERICAN SHIPS (Barre Gazette, Barre, Mass., 1962).

Hay, M. D. (Ed.), LANDSMAN HAY, MEMOIRS OF ROBERT HAY, 1789–1847 (Rupert Hart-Davis, London, 1953).

Hayet, Capt. A., CHANSONS DE BORD (Éditions Eos, Paris, 1927).

Hugill, Stan, SHANTIES FROM THE SEVEN SEAS (Routledge & Kegan Paul Ltd, London, 1961).

Huntington, Gale, SONGS THE WHALEMEN SANG (Barre Publishers, Barre, Mass., 1964).

Ives, Burl, SEA SONGS (Ballantyne Books Inc., New York, 1956).

Ives, Burl, THE BURL IVES SONG BOOK (Ballantyne Books Inc., New York, 1953).

Jenson, Oscar, INTERNATIONALE SØMANDS-OPSANGE (Copenhagen, 1923).

JOURNAL OF THE FOLK SONG SOCIETY, 1899–1931. Published by the Folk Song Society, London (Shanties and Sea-songs collected by Miss Gilchrist, H. E. Piggott, Percy Grainger, Hon. Ed. Fielding, C. J. Sharp, W. J. Alden, Margaret Harley, Thomas Miners, J. E. Thomas, etc.).

King, S. H., KING'S BOOK OF CHANTIES (Oliver Ditson Co., Boston, 1918).

Le Bihor, Jean-Marie, CHANSONS DE LA VOILE, "SANS VOILES" (Dunkirk, 1935). This is a pseudonym for Capt. A. Hayet.

Lomax, John A., and Alan Lomax, OUR SINGING COUNTRY (Macmillan Co., New York, 1941).

Lomax, John A., and Alan Lomax, AMERICAN BALLADS AND FOLK SONGS (Macmillan, 1934; reprinted 1961).

Luce, Admiral S. B., NAVAL SONGS (W. A. Pond & Co., New York, 1883).

Mackenzie, R. W., BALLADS AND SEA SONGS FROM NOVA SCOTIA (Harvard University Press, Cambridge, Mass., 1928).

Masefield, John, A SAILOR'S GARLAND (London, 1924).

Nordhoff, Charles, THE MERCHANT VESSEL (Dodd, Mead & Co., New York, 1884).

Olmstead, F. A., INCIDENTS OF A WHALING VOYAGE (D. Appleton & Co., New York, 1841).

Patterson, J. E., THE SEA'S ANTHOLOGY (G. H. Doran, New York, 1913).

Robinson, Capt. John, "Songs of the Chantey Man", THE BELLMAN (Minneapolis, Minn., 14 July to 4 August 1917).

ROXBURGHE BALLADS (9 vols., the Ballads Society, Hertford, 1871-99) Edited by W. Chappell & J. W. Ebsworth.

Samson, John, THE SEVEN SEAS SHANTY BOOK (Boosey & Co. Ltd, London, 1927).

Sandburg, Carl, THE AMERICAN SONGBAG (Harcourt, Brace & Co., New York, 1927).

Sharp, Cecil J., ENGLISH FOLK-CHANTEYS (Simkin Marshall Ltd, Schott & Co. Ltd, London, 1914).

Shaw, Capt. Frank, THE SPLENDOUR OF THE SEAS (Edward Stanford Ltd, London, 1953).

Shay, Frank, IRON MEN AND WOODEN SHIPS (Doubleday, Page & Co., New York, 1924).

Shay, Frank, AMERICAN SEA SONGS AND CHANTEYS (W. W. Norton & Co. Inc., New York, 1948).

SHELL BOOK OF SHANTIES, THE (Shell Petroleum Co. Ltd, London, 1952).

Smith, C. Fox, A BOOK OF SHANTIES (Methuen & Co. Ltd, London, 1927).

Smith, Laura A., THE MUSIC OF THE WATERS (Kegan Paul, Trench & Co., London, 1888).

"Steerage Passenger", THE QUID, OR TALES OF MY MESSMATES (W. Strange, London, 1832).

Sternvall, Capt. S., SÅNG UNDER SEGAL (Albert Bonniers Forlag, Stockholm, 1935).

Stone, Christopher, SEA SONGS AND BALLADS (Clarendon Press, Oxford, 1906).

Terry, R. R., THE SHANTY BOOK, two parts (J. Curwen & Sons Ltd, London, 1931).

Terry, R. R., SALT SEA BALLADS (J. Curwen & Sons Ltd, London, 1931).

Whall, Capt. W. B., SEA SONGS AND SHANTIES (first edition called SHIPS, SEA SONGS AND SHANTIES, 1910) (Brown, Son and Ferguson Ltd, Glasgow, 1927).

Whitehead, A. W., and S. T. Harris, SIX SEA SHANTIES (Boosey & Co. Ltd, London, 1925).

INDEX

243